P9-CFX-713

3 9077 08826 6112

"In *The #MeToo Reckoning*, Rev. Ruth Everhart takes the church to have been an abysmal response to sexual abuse behind its closed doors. Laying out proof of the abuse of the most vulnerable among us in the place that should be the most safe, she gives suggestions for how pastors, congregations, and the church at-large can begin to serve everyone through openness, victim support, and use of the legal system. With an unapologetic voice, she calls for the protection of individuals from predators who have too easily been not only allowed to serve but also protected by spiritual leadership from pastors up through the highest liturgical powers that be. With personal experiences detailed as well as those of other pastors, *The #MeToo Reckoning* is an engaging, thoughtful, and necessary book in these times that Jesus asks of his church, 'What will you do with me?'"

Lisa Samson, author of *Quaker Summer, The Church Ladies,* and *Love Mercy*

"Ruth Everhart writes with great insight and passion. She shines a steady, penetrating light on sexual abuse in the church. Alas, this book is entirely necessary."

Neal Plantinga, author of *Not the Way It's Supposed to Be: A Breviary of Sin*

"This is a book for survivors, for churches who have failed victims, for those who seek to mourn with those who mourn, and for those who love justice and endeavor to bring healing and renewal. By weaving together biblical narratives and contemporary stories with her own painful past, Ruth Everhart unflinchingly confronts the culture of silence, shame, and denial that too often characterizes a Christian response to abuse. This is a book of reckoning."

Kristin Kobes Du Mez, professor of history and gender studies at Calvin College, author of *A New Gospel for Women*

"In her remarkable clarion call for change, Ruth Everhart reminds religious leaders tempted to view #MeToo as a dismissible modern political movement that variations of 'me too' have echoed off the walls of the church since its foundation. This book begs us all to answer the question: How much longer will we shut our ears to the voice of God heard in the cries of the 'the least of these'?"

Linda Kay Klein, author of *Pure: Inside the Evangelical Movement That Shamed a Generation of Young Women and How I Broke Free*

"Individual bodies can't heal until they receive a diagnosis. Likewise, the body of Christ can't heal until it learns what is making it sick. With bold storytelling and deep engagement with the biblical text, Ruth Everhart diagnoses the unchecked power, patriarchy, and shallow forms of forgiveness that plague many Christian communities grappling with abuse. She also points to the cure: a better, more biblical practice of justice for victims. May this book ensure that more victims' cries for justice are finally heard."

Katelyn Beaty, author of *A Woman's Place: A Christian Vision for Your Calling in the Office, the Home, and the World*

"In *The #MeToo Reckoning*, Ruth Everhart creatively interweaves real-life stories of how Protestant churches have been complicit in the sexual abuse of women with counterpart stories from Scripture. In telling the stories—both the real-life stories and the biblical ones—Everhart does not flinch from pointing out how those who held the reins of power used silence, evasion, threats, and denial to protect abusers. In each case, she goes beyond denunciation, however, to point out how they could and should have acted differently. The result is a gripping, prophetic call to churches to halt the cover-ups of sexual abuse of women and secure justice for the victims. An eloquent, spiritually deep wake-up call. This book had to be written!"

Nicholas Wolterstorff, Noah Porter Professor Emeritus of Philosophical Theology, Yale University

"The church must pay attention to the #MeToo movement. Among us are victims of sexual abuse who have been marginalized and perpetrators who have received easy grace. Through case studies and a careful look at Scripture, Ruth Everhart helps us understand the religious and cultural dynamics that foster sexual violence against women and children. I highly recommend *The #MeToo Reckoning* as a resource for congregations committed to preventing and confronting sexual violence."

Nancy Werking Poling, editor of *Victim to Survivor: Women Recovering from Clergy Sexual Abuse*

"Throughout the Bible, the wrath of God is directed toward injustice. In *The #MeToo Reckoning*, Ruth Everhart shows that the church deserves God's wrath for its complicity in sexual abuse and misconduct. In a personal, pastoral, and prophetic way, she explores the depth of the problem, connects it to Scripture, and offers us a needed way forward."

Henry G. Brinton, Presbyterian pastor and author of the novel *City of Peace*

"I am deeply grateful for Ruth Everhart and her timely work. *The #MeToo Reckoning* bears witness to the pain Everhart and others have experienced as survivors of sexual assault, affirming that women's voices need to be heard—and affirmed—if churches want to create safe spaces where girls and women can thrive. I am especially grateful for Everhart's work at dismantling the patriarchal structures, systemic and otherwise, that have allowed some to continue abusing others without reprisal. And I appreciate Everhart's careful consideration of Scripture and her insistence that Jesus longs for his people to end sexual assault in all its manifestations. In a time when #MeToo survivors are numberless, this is the good news we need to hear."

Melanie Springer Mock, professor of English at George Fox University and author of *Worthy: Finding Yourself in a World Expecting Someone Else*

"In *The #MeToo Reckoning*, Ruth Everhart shines a fierce light on the ways churches have been complacent or complicit in dismissing and diminishing victims of sexual malfeasance. Everhart's hard-won insights into the ways church leadership has failed to protect against the wolves in our fold make this book challenging but necessary reading for pastors and laity alike."
David Williams, pastor and author of *When the English Fall*

"Like the prophets before her, Ruth Everhart has a piercing, lucid, and urgent message: as long as the church idolizes power—the power of the institution or the lone charismatic leader, success, or patriarchal masculinity; as long as it holds up the strong at the expense of the vulnerable—it fails in its mission. Though this is not an easy book, it is ultimately hopeful, revealing with practical and concrete wisdom, a path forward. The work is suffused with inspired and delightfully original readings of biblical texts."
Debbie Blue, pastor and author of *Consider the Women: A Provocative Guide to Three Matriarchs of the Bible*

"This book shouldn't need to exist. It's a difficult read, not because of the writing, which is heartbreakingly eloquent, but because of the subject: the abuse within the body of Christ that is at the same time sexual and spiritual. Through wise exposition of Scripture, Ruth Everhart challenges religious institutions as places where abuse is too often discounted, denied, and concealed. I applaud the brave souls who share their stories of pain, including Everhart, and for her courageous call for change that is healing and just. May her wisdom hasten the day when there are no more such stories to tell."
Kathleen Long Bostrom, author and retired minister

"Ruth Everhart's writing is genuine prophetic speech. It not only uproots, it also plants. Her voice helps unmask a system that has kept women in the shadows for too long. At the same time, her pastoral heart helps heal, touch, and encourage thriving survivors like me. *The #MeToo Reckoning* reminds us that justice is knocking at the door and asks us, *How will you respond?*"
Jeanette Salguero, associate pastor and COO of Calvario City Church, senior vice president of the National Latino Evangelical Coalition

"*The #MeToo Reckoning* should be required reading for all church leaders. Everhart gives churches precisely what they need—practical solutions for preventing and responding to abuse. Through powerful storytelling and insightful scriptural analysis, Everhart shows how we got where we are, why abuse matters, and how the church can find a way forward. This book has the power to promote real change."
Jen Zamzow, adjunct faculty at Concordia University Irvine

"Ruth Everhart knows and understands firsthand as a survivor and a pastor that all too often Christian communities are quick to dismiss and marginalize those who have been abused within their midst while at the same time empowering (and sometimes celebrating) those who abuse. Her unique confrontation with this dark reality provides Ruth with a much-needed perspective that the church must hear and learn from if we genuinely love and follow the Jesus we profess to love and follow. We are fortunate to have such a voice of wisdom in our midst who is also a tremendously gifted communicator. *The #MeToo Reckoning* is a critical warning shot across the bow of Christendom that I pray will help wake us up before it's too late."

Boz Tchividjian, abuse attorney and founder, GRACE

"Ruth Everhart has given the church an amazing gift: truth, courage, and hope for a way forward. What a powerful resource for faith leaders everywhere!"

Anna Carter Florence, Peter Marshall Professor of Preaching, Columbia Theological Seminary

THE
#MeToo
RECKONING

FACING THE CHURCH'S COMPLICITY
IN SEXUAL ABUSE AND MISCONDUCT

RUTH
EVERHART

An imprint of InterVarsity Press
Downers Grove, Illinois

InterVarsity Press
P.O. Box 1400, Downers Grove, IL 60515-1426
ivpress.com
email@ivpress.com

©2020 by Ruth H. Everhart

All rights reserved. No part of this book may be reproduced in any form without written permission from InterVarsity Press.

InterVarsity Press® is the book-publishing division of InterVarsity Christian Fellowship/USA®, a movement of students and faculty active on campus at hundreds of universities, colleges, and schools of nursing in the United States of America, and a member movement of the International Fellowship of Evangelical Students. For information about local and regional activities, visit intervarsity.org.

Scripture quotations, unless otherwise noted, are from the New Revised Standard Version of the Bible, copyright 1989 by the Division of Christian Education of the National Council of the Churches of Christ in the USA. Used by permission. All rights reserved.

While any stories in this book are true, some names and identifying information may have been changed to protect the privacy of individuals.

The author is represented by MacGregor Literary, Inc.

Cover design and image composite: David Fassett
Interior design: Daniel van Loon
Images: empty church: © Joel Carillet / E+ / Getty Images

ISBN 978-0-8308-4582-8 (print)
ISBN 978-0-8308-4943-7 (digital)

Printed in the United States of America ♾

InterVarsity Press is committed to ecological stewardship and to the conservation of natural resources in all our operations. This book was printed using sustainably sourced paper.

Library of Congress Cataloging-in-Publication Data
A catalog record for this book is available from the Library of Congress.

P   25   24   23   22   21   20   19   18   17   16   15   14   13   12   11   10   9   8   7   6   5   4   3   2   1
Y   41   40   39   38   37   36   35   34   33   32   31   30   29   28   27   26   25   24   23   22   21   20

TO ALL SURVIVORS OF SEXUAL ABUSE

and the faith communities who care for you

Have I now become your enemy by telling you the truth?

GALATIANS 4:16

For nothing is hidden that will not be disclosed, nor is anything secret that will not become known and come to light.

LUKE 8:17

There is no act, no sermon, no parable in the whole Gospel that borrows its pungency from female perversity; nobody could possibly guess from the words and deeds of Jesus that there was anything "funny" about woman's nature. But we might easily deduce it from . . . His Church to this day. Women are not human; nobody shall persuade that they are human.

DOROTHY L. SAYERS, "THE HUMAN-NOT-QUITE-HUMAN"

CONTENTS

PREFACE

TO MY READERS

If you're a victim whose life is still colored by the abuse you suffered, I'm grateful you would dare to read these pages. This act affirms how courageous you are, how determined to find wholeness. Not only does Jesus love you, but I also held you in my mind and heart as I wrote.

If you're a survivor—meaning that you've reclaimed a sense of wholeness and largely moved on from abuse you've suffered —I hope these pages remind you that you are not alone and inspire you to raise your voice within your relationships, especially within your church. Let us together become a chorus that cannot be silenced.

If you seek to be an ally, a special welcome. It takes effort to view the world through the lens of a victim or survivor, an effort that pays off. I hope the stories told here, and the uniquely female lens on Scripture, will enlarge your vision and inspire action.

If you're a pastor, I hope you find inspiration as you minister to the abused—and the abusers—who fill church pews. I hope these pages provide fodder for preaching, resources for discussion, encouragement to prosecute abusers, and the means to make your congregation a safer and braver space.

If you're a lay leader, I would like to shake your hand. When people who love the church—but are not paid to do so—are willing to spend their time and energy listening to survivors and confronting abusers, that gives me optimism for the future of the church. My hopes for you are identical to those for pastors since clergy and lay lead as partners.

If you're not a Christian, my sincere thanks for picking up this book. I hope you hear the call to justice that underlies the gospel message—a call too often obscured by the church's complacent merger with American culture. Jesus is not a mild-natured fella who blesses the power brokers. Jesus passionately supports all those who are treated as *less than*, including women.

I encourage all of you to reach out with stories, reactions, and next steps. The About the Author page at the end lists ways to be in touch.

> **WARNING**
>
> This book contains graphic descriptions of sexual harassment and sexual violence, which may be triggering to survivors.

INTRODUCTION

O LORD, *how long shall I cry for help,*
   and you will not listen?
Or cry to you "Violence!"
   and you will not save?

HABAKKUK 1:2

LIKE THE PROPHETS OF OLD, victims of sexual assault cry out for justice. Their voices have been amplified by the #MeToo movement, which is passing through culture like a freight train, its momentum toppling once-powerful men from high positions. To some, the movement may be rattling, disquieting, and unnerving, but to survivors, the movement is exhilarating, empowering, and long overdue.

The phrase "Me Too" was coined in 2006 by the civil rights activist Tarana Burke to lift up the prevalence of sexual assault. It became a viral hashtag in 2017 when allegations against prominent film producer Harvey Weinstein roared through the media. Others tweeted their own #MeToo stories, and the rumble created reverberations that could no longer be ignored. As story after story splashed across front pages, the uncomfortable truth resounded: women are so frequently abused because they are seen as *less than* men—less worthy, less valuable, less valued.

In courtrooms and board rooms, abusers began to face consequences that were previously unknown: job loss, jail time, or career implosion. As the media amplified the voices of victims, corporate culture sat up and took notice. The worlds of entertainment and sports, whose profits depend on viewers, adjusted to the new norms.

But where is the church? Instead of exposing wrongdoing and calling for justice, it is too often the culprit. Even worse, it's the place where culpability hides.

WHY I WROTE THIS BOOK

I didn't choose to spend years of my life pondering sexual abuse and faith. As painful topics so often do, this topic chose me. Many of the stories in these pages are connected to my own life. The recurring motif of sexual assault began in 1978 when I was a senior at a conservative Christian college in Michigan. Two armed intruders broke into the off-campus house I shared with four housemates. The criminals held us hostage at gunpoint for six hours. They robbed us, then raped us. Those hours of point-blank brutality and terror stopped my life—not only the end of a sentence but the close of a paragraph, a chapter.[1]

Because my conservative religious upbringing taught that women should guard their sexual purity above all else, I believed that being raped had damaged me beyond repair. I struggled with feelings of shame and worthlessness. It took a decade to recover my sense of self and rebuild a new sort of faith, one that took evil into account.

The circumstances of our case were unusual because they were so clear-cut: the criminals broke in while we were asleep;

they were armed; they were serial offenders. In addition, they were African American men who targeted white women. While it's painful to realize that the assailants' race was likely a factor, I will forever be grateful that the investigation and prosecution were vigorous and successful.[2] That makes our case unusual in an almost astronomical sense—one of *point zero five percent* (0.05 percent) of all rapes ends in conviction.[3] For me, testifying before a jury was a healing balm, an experience of empowerment. I'm an advocate for survivors because the world needs to hear our voices. Our stories are powerful. I told mine because so many of you cannot tell yours, at least not yet.

Unfortunately, my religious community was not as helpful or healing as the justice system. In our Christian campus bubble, very few people reached out. When I approached pastors and professors, they were unable to answer my theological questions. I was told to "put it behind me and move on." I wasn't even sure what "it" was: the violence? the trauma? my status as a good girl? the fact that my life's underpinnings had been wiped out in the space of six hours?

I felt alienated and furious as well as traumatized. I'd been trained for pleasantness, not for the fury that now coursed through me—for good reason. Not only had my happy future been wrenched away, but everything I believed to be certain was actually tenuous.

Still, I discovered that the psalmist spoke the truth: "The LORD is near to the brokenhearted, / and saves the crushed in spirit" (Psalm 34:18). Jesus was relentless in drawing me close. Over the next decade, despite my questions—or perhaps through them—I discerned a call to ministry. After I met and married my husband, Doug, I applied to seminary. Those four

years of classes and internships were life-changing. By graduation day, I was pregnant with our second daughter and full of
plans for a rebuilt future.

I supply this background to be transparent about my approach. My interest in sexual assault and faith is not academic.
I wrote this book because I felt called by God to do so and
could find no excuse to refuse (although I did search for one).
I bring certain lenses along with me. As a rape survivor, I am
passionate about justice for victims and accountability for victimizers. As a former "good girl," I am conversant with the
conservative subculture. As a committed Christian, I am tena-
cious about loving Jesus, who first loved me. As a pastor, I
spend my days swimming in Scripture. As a wife, I am one half
of what turned out to be an egalitarian marriage, thirty-five
years and counting. As a mother, my heart walks around
outside my body with two daughters, a fact that will keep me
poking and prodding the church toward greater gender equality
as long as I live. Most of all, as an author, the response to my
earlier writing about assault has softened my heart and
thickened my skin. I will not be bullied by blowback or made
callous to the plight of my sister survivors and brothers as well.
It is time for a reckoning.

Let me be clear about another thing: I am not a liberal feminist. I am a radical feminist. Which is to say, it's not enough
that individual women can thrive in a patriarchal culture. As
long as women as a group are treated as *less than* men, it doesn't
matter that individual women can experience success. Inequality is not what God intends for human society.

Inequality is certainly not what Jesus modeled. My love for
Jesus is why I embrace the #MeToo movement. As imperfect

as it is, this collective action highlights the ways that inequality breeds abuse. It has garnered the power to push back against that abuse, pushback that is long overdue. I feel frustrated when Christians treat #MeToo as a sinful movement dripping with the venom of feminism. Feminism is not a hateful ideology. It's the belief that women are people too.

WHY EQUALITY MATTERS

Men can be sexually assaulted, but women are disproportionately victimized. One out of every six women is the victim of an attempted or completed rape in her lifetime.[4] The fact that children are often victims presents a host of special considerations for the church. It's also important to acknowledge that people of color suffer higher levels of sexual assault than whites. More people are enslaved now than at any previous time in human history, thanks to a growing global sex trade.[5] Most of these victims are people of color, and the majority are children. In the United States, the preponderance of victims of color is due to our nation's legacy of race-based slavery, which treated African Americans as subhuman for four centuries. Crimes against victims with brown or black skin continue to be viewed more dispassionately than are crimes against white victims, while crimes committed by people of color are prosecuted more vigorously than are crimes by whites. Our justice system reflects these imbalances in its rates of apprehension, prosecution, and incarceration.[6]

#MeToo is not a women's issue; it's a human issue. It's not a feminist movement; it's a justice movement. If churches will link arms with this liberating work, our faith communities can become places of healing. Since Christians worship a God who created all persons, who seeks to redeem all, and whose Spirit is available to all, it would make sense that they would rally around a movement to eradicate the sin of sexual assault. But when it comes to protecting the vulnerable and prosecuting offenders, the sad truth is that churches are no better than our culture at large. Many would say that churches are actually worse—that they are places of increased sexism and misogyny.

Sexism and *misogyny* are often treated as fighting words. I use them descriptively. Kate Manne suggests that sexism is an offshoot of patriarchal ideology, justifying and rationalizing a male-dominant social order, while misogyny is the system that polices and enforces these norms.[7] In other words, sexism is a "logical" system springing from the belief that males should be dominant, whereas misogyny is the heat and emotion that powers this thinking and creates backlash when it is opposed. Manne summarizes, "Sexism is scientific; misogyny is moralistic."[8]

These definitions are recent, but the reality they try to pin down is anything but. Christians have to grapple with the fact that Jesus was born into a misogynistic culture and ministered in the middle of it. Our own times are not much more enlightened. Women are still treated as *less than* men in ways large and small. The price of patriarchy is sexual abuse, and people who love Jesus should no longer be willing to accept that anyone should pay that price. The church has been too slow to connect the assumptions of patriarchy with the realities of sexual abuse. I pray that nothing—not even a recalcitrant church—can hold back the tide that's calling our culture to account.

I believe that Jesus is part of the #MeToo movement, whether or not the church is at his side. The spirit of Jesus is always on the move when people rise up for equality and justice. And Jesus is never lacking for partners, though some of the partners might surprise us. If Christians won't join arms, then those in entertainment, sports, business, and politics will lead the way, if only for the sake of their bottom line. I'm sure Jesus welcomes these partners. Still, I have to think he's happy when the people who bear his name join him in the work of ending sexual assault.

THE S*ITUATION

Because I have become a progressive Protestant, this book focuses on stories within that world. I feel a call to clean the dirt in my own house, rather than to chastise my neighbors. Still, we are all affected by the cumulative weight of the "s*ituation"— the abuse and assault revelations that appear with regularity. Every flavor of Christian faith has been sullied, from Catholic to conservative Protestant to so-called mainline Protestant. The sexual abuse and cover-up within the global Roman Catholic Church has forever changed that enormous body. Prominent leaders in large evangelical churches are facing their own #MeToo accusations. These include Bill Hybels (Willow Creek Church), Andy Savage (Highpoint Church), Paige Patterson (Southwestern Baptist Theological Seminary), and Bill Gothard (Institute in Basic Life Principles).[9] A February 2019 article in the *Houston Chronicle* exposed a sweeping story of "20 years, 700 victims" within the Southern Baptist Convention.[10] These stories involve child victims. Other conservative leaders such as C. J. Mahaney (Sovereign Grace Ministries) and Brian Houston (Hillsong Church) face allegations of covering up sexual abuse.[11]

Each new revelation triggers shock waves that ripple through faith communities and through the faith of each member. Who and what can we trust? On a societal level, the word *church* no longer means *trustworthy*, not even for true believers. Churches must confront this hard reality. The trust they betrayed can never be rebuilt. Instead—and only if they address the extent of the betrayal—faith leaders can begin to build trust anew. This is a long-term and costly proposition, so buckle up. Churches can take specific steps to address abuse, which I'll sketch in the final chapter.

BECAUSE JESUS

Why not let secular society continue to lead the way in #MeToo? Because of Jesus. Even people who don't know Jesus well know that he came back to life after he died. It's what he's famous for. But do we know what he said when he came back to life? The first word on his lips was "Woman" (John 20:15). Women not only attended Jesus' death, they were the first to witness his resurrection. Jesus entrusted his most precious gift—his message—to the care and keeping of women (see Matthew 28:9-10, Mark 16:9-11, Luke 24:10). This, despite the fact that a woman's testimony carried no legal weight during that time.

Such an unlikely act tells us something essential about Jesus. He chose to live outside the culture's limitations and calls us to do the same. Jesus treated women as having the same value and worth as men. To Jesus, women were created in the image of God, which has no gender and endows humans with moral agency.

While I don't mean to recast Jesus in my own image—he was a first-century Jewish rabbi, not a post-modern feminist—

he disregarded many of the conventions of his day. He treated women—and every sick, deformed, or *less than* person—with respect. Despite religious prohibitions against it, Jesus approached women and engaged them in lengthy conversations (see Mark 7:24-30). When women who needed healing sought him out and touched him, Jesus did not reprimand them. Sometimes he even initiated the healing touch. By his word and touch, Jesus freed women from sickness, ostracism, and death.

I am completely convinced that if Jesus walked on earth today, he would push back against the systems that oppress women still. It would seem to follow that people who say they love Jesus would be champions of women, but that is rarely the case. Too often, Christians have been complicit in championing a patriarchal masculinity that marginalizes women and protects abusers.

TELLING STORIES

Since the stories we tell have the power to change cultural norms, this book invites you to explore two types of stories around sexual assault. Half are current stories, and half are from Scripture. I hope you can hear them in tandem, the twin halves of a double helix. Comparing the stories will both challenge and change us.

The biblical stories come from both testaments of Scripture. Each story's context assumes that women are not of equal value to men. While that shouldn't surprise anyone who has studied the Bible, the repercussions can still shock us.

The current stories shine a light on the prevalence of sexual abuse within faith communities. Of the eight stories I tell, four are interlinked with my own. A fifth is from a church I know well. The other three come from courageous survivors, two women and one man. I did not seek out these stories; they were entrusted to me.

Each of the current stories took place within a Protestant context, though the congregations ranged from conservative to liberal. Where a congregation falls on that spectrum matters, and it's worth identifying how and why. Many conservative churches exercise prohibitions against women in leadership and believe that the genders have distinctly different, God-given roles. This attachment to gender inequality is not some easily dismissible sliver of Christianity. Rather, this viewpoint is so dominant that, to many people, a "Christian" is someone who believes that God created women to be subservient to men.

Conservative churches apply a particular understanding to the word translated as *helpmate* in the second creation story (see Genesis 2:18). While the Hebrew word *ezer* means strength and is mostly applied to God, conservatives believe that *ezer kenegdo,* when applied to woman, signals subordination and relegates her to a "complementary" role in marriage, home, church, and society.

While complementarians insist that these gendered roles are equal in value, in practice they are not. From my childhood, I know that the roles do not *feel* equal. Certainly the dynamic created is one of unequal power. This is an enormous problem. Sexual abuse is always the abuse of power. I am not alone in connecting the dots between a conservative view of gender roles and increased harm from sexual abuse.[12]

THE AMOEBA

It takes faith to believe that alternatives exist to the unequal and often violent world in which we live, but we find inspiration in Jesus' example. In the Gospel of Luke, Jesus notices a woman so beat down by the world that she is literally bent over (see Luke 13:11). Who else but Jesus would notice an unnoticeable woman? Remember that the crowd always surrounds Jesus like a giant amoeba, the edges constantly shifting but the center always coalescing around him, the nucleus. Every sick, deformed, or overworked person in Palestine wanted to be near the Teacher. Amid the pressed bodies and pressing agendas of the Jesus-amoeba, he notices a bent-over woman. What's more, he *sees* her. He doesn't see an invalid, a drain on the system—a worthless woman. He sees a child of God who needs to be lifted up.

We must do as Jesus did and dare to notice, see, listen, and engage. This is risky business. To open our eyes to the lived experience of women is to open our eyes to abuse. But faithfulness impels us to open them, and also our hearts, minds, and perspectives. We might even call this new vision an inbreaking of the kingdom of God.

THE RECKONING

The #MeToo movement may be current news, but what it protests is not new. Sexual assault is as old as Scripture. Only particular forms of exposure and accountability are new: the hashtags, the social media, the front page coverage. It may be new that some powerful men have faced public consequences, but the struggle for justice after sexual assault is an old story. Others have engaged this struggle, and we stand on their shoulders, grateful. All justice work is incremental, with each generation bringing new vision. #MeToo is focusing attention on how far society still must go before we achieve gender equality. Only then will the occurrence of sexual abuse be reduced, because abuse thrives and hides where power is imbalanced. Lady Justice—with her blindfolded eyes, scales, and sword—has known this all along.

Real change is disruptive. Some churches act as if they're waiting for the #MeToo freight train to pass. Some leaders pretend they're giving institutions time to respond. But to stand idle is to abdicate our responsibility as Jesus followers. We are each responsible for the historical inch we occupy. It's my conviction that this #MeToo inch is a gift to churches, one we are too slow to receive.

I call on people of faith to embrace the reckoning of the #MeToo movement. We must recognize that God's presence strengthens each victim who finally feels empowered to tell the truth; that Jesus stands in sorrow with victims and in judgment with victimizers, especially those who refuse to confess their sin; and that the Spirit calls each of us to confess the ways we have normalized violence against the vulnerable. Now we are to lament, repent, and participate in a new vision of equality and justice.

The church can listen to survivors' stories, study our Scripture for lessons on gender and abuse, and dare to apply what we learn to change church culture. We will unburden victims and survivors, removing the load of shame we have allowed to land on their shoulders, which has increased the evil done to them. We will hold predatory pastors and members accountable. We will make our churches both safer and braver.

This reckoning will take a stout heart and strong stomach. And it will cost us. Exposing our dark past may cost our churches their reputations and cultural authority—if they have any left. But Jesus says, "Those who want to save their life will lose it, and those who lose their life for my sake, and for the sake of the gospel, will save it" (Mark 8:35). Churches may need to lose many things, even everything. Let's hope that churches lose the right things: an addiction to cultural power and authority, a self-righteous clamp on the idol of sexual purity, an attachment to secrecy and silence as effective means of control. I pray that these things will wash away as the power of Jesus captures another generation.

As it always does. As it cannot *not*.

The Jesus we follow is like no other. His love changes everything. He is the divine one who came into this world via vagina. To Jesus, women's bodily experiences matter. To Jesus, all humans bear the image of God equally. To Jesus, the voices of victims crying out for justice is a beatitude sung by a chorus.

Stop and listen. Push past the fear. Unleash the energy. The Spirit is here.

CHAPTER ONE

POWER AND PATRIARCHY

Men are afraid that women will laugh at them.
Women are afraid that men will kill them.

MARGARET ATWOOD

No, my brother, do not force me; for such a thing is
not done in Israel; do not do anything so vile!

2 SAMUEL 13:12

NOT FAR INTO MY FIRST YEAR of seminary, I began to wonder

whether I would make it after all. The four-year program had already begun to feel like a marathon—and I'm not a runner.

I was earning a master of divinity degree, which would equip me to receive a call to a church and be ordained as a minister of word and sacrament in the Presbyterian Church (USA). Every part of seminary, from the heady subject matter and interminable readings to the demanding internships, felt all-consuming. Seminary seemed *designed* to consume us, or at least to consume every sure thing we brought with us: the childhood beliefs, the rote creeds, the heartfelt but unexamined convictions. These had to be examined and dismantled so that new beliefs could be constructed. By graduation, we would have presumably *mastered the divine.*

Judy, an older friend who had graduated and received a call to a ministry position, invited me to her ordination. I attended to see what it looked like to cross the finish line. The service took place on a Sunday evening in a beautiful, old church in a Minneapolis neighborhood. The vaulted sanctuary had long, curving pews in dark wood and a sloping floor. Organ music reverberated as a half-dozen participants dressed in black robes and colorful stoles proceeded down the center aisle. The service brimmed with songs, Scripture, and solemn vows in a mood both festive and serious. I drank it in. A seminary graduation confers a diploma, a sheepskin, but ordination confers a status, the standing of shepherd. My classmate would no longer be just Judy but *reverend*.

The pursuit of that title—at the time a forbidden status for women—had brought me to seminary. The Christian Reformed Church, the church of my childhood, barred women from entering ministry.[1] I felt this as a deeply personal affront. To my Dutch forebears, the fact that I was female meant ordination was verboten. That I felt the call of God did not matter. Whether I was smart enough, skilled enough, or disciplined enough was irrelevant. The door was shut. So I enrolled at a more liberal seminary. My professors were welcoming, but I encountered internal barriers: *Who was I fooling? I didn't deserve to be here. I would never make it.*

That evening at my friend's ordination, my whirling emotions found an anchor in the black pulpit robe presented to her as a gift. Judy would don it officially for the first time after the laying on of hands to signify that she had become Reverend Rhodes. I knew that some pastors wore such robes, but not in my tradition, where preachers wore dark suits and white shirts, the conservative attire of powerful men. A pulpit robe struck me as outdated and ungainly. Even ridiculous. A preacher couldn't so much as fill a water glass without those flapping sleeves getting wet. How nerve-racking to walk up chancel steps with all that cloth fluttering around your feet. But for all those limitations—maybe *because* of them—the robe declared its power. It was not designed to be handy, or useful, or particularly beautiful. It was designed to convey that the wearer had entered a rarefied profession, adding power and authority to the preaching of the Word.

The ordination service was nearing its climax. Judy knelt and the black-robed participants clustered around her, each laying a hand on her head and shoulders. An authority figure prayed for the Spirit to descend upon her. Watching, I felt a flood of awe, a frisson of fear. Power was present, undeniably— but also danger.

To me, the ordination felt as mysterious as the practice of alchemy. An ordinary mortal had been transformed into a minister before my eyes. It didn't occur to me then—or for decades afterward—that the ritual of ordination might be considered, in some sense, a way of joining the patriarchy, of donning the power of a certain status.

PATRIARCHY

I was five years old in 1963, the year Betty Friedan published her seminal work *The Feminine Mystique.* What she called "the problem that has no name"[2] described the shared female experience of being *less than* men, of being given a very limited role to occupy. Friedan's work spurred women to become conscious of patriarchy. Seven years later, Robin Morgan edited an anthology

FAIR... ...LIBRARY
1 FAIRPORT VILLAGE LANDING
FAIRPORT NY 14450

of radical feminist writings that included the voices of women of color titled *Sisterhood Is Powerful: An Anthology of Writings from the Women's Liberation Movement*.[3] Morgan's work highlighted the systemic nature of women's oppression in the workplace and political system. This not only raised consciousness but also called people to push back against patriarchy.

Loosely defined, the word *patriarchy* refers to laws that keep males in power, ranging across systems of governance in the nation, state, business, church, and family. Across the millennia, men's legal rights—to vote, hold office, own a business, buy property, and pass property on to male heirs—ensured that men had access to power that women lacked. Patriarchal laws also ensured that white men had access to power that men of color lacked, creating the racial disparities that afflict America today. Since the fruit of patriarchy is injustice, patriarchy is sinful.

Included in patriarchy are traditions and norms that don't carry the force of law but rely on longstanding habit and common practice. These often linger longer than laws. Examples are a wife taking her husband's name, a husband expecting his wife to shoulder the housework, or referring to a father's portion of childcare as "babysitting."

Patriarchal laws and norms descended from antiquity, so they color the stories we read in Scripture. These "biblical norms" are often used to defend today's patriarchal norms. Certainly, they shaped the way I was raised. To be a "good girl" meant being silent, docile, and obedient. In my home, church, and private Christian school, it was assumed that males would wield the power. After all, the pattern of male dominance and female compliance was dictated by Scripture.

SETTING THE STAGE: TAMAR'S STORY

If it didn't involve incest in a royal family, the story of Tamar in 2 Samuel 13 would seem commonplace: a powerful man targets a beautiful woman, deceives her, traps her, overpowers her, sexually assaults her, and then casts her aside as worthless. Had Tamar been a nameless woman, her story would have been lost to history, as so many others undoubtedly have been.

But Tamar is the daughter of David, a towering biblical figure, the shepherd boy who killed the giant Goliath with a slingshot and was anointed king. Because of her proximity to the throne, Tamar's story is riddled with palace intrigue. Amnon, her assailant, is also her half-brother and first in line to David's throne. Absalom, her "rescuer," is her full brother and second in line to the throne. When Absalom avenged Tamar's assault, years later, his action not only altered the line of succession but made him king. This is probably the reason Scripture records the story.

Even though Tamar has the power of a royal name, the story of her rape ends up being less about *her* and more about her brothers vying for power. These dynamics—both of power and vulnerability—are captured in a rare textual detail about her clothing, a "long robe with sleeves; for this is how the virgin daughters of the king were clothed" (2 Samuel 13:18). It's fitting that Tamar laments her assault by tearing the robe that defines her place.

SETTING THE STAGE: MY STORY

When I graduated from seminary, my husband, Doug, was finishing his teaching credentials, our daughter was a toddler, and I was pregnant with number two. As soon as our second daughter was born, I called the headquarters of the Presbyterian Church (USA) and requested the list of churches with open positions. While my infant nursed I pored through the computer printouts. Each listing contained a possible new future.

Doug and I were more than ready to become professionals and leave our student juggling act behind. For years, we had passed everything back and forth between us like a four-handed circus performance: three part-time jobs, two sets of professional coursework, and one rattletrap car—not to mention taking care of our daughters. We dreamed of the day our family would be settled in a place where he could teach and I could preach. I purposely cast a wide net of applications, feeling excited to entertain a dozen dreams at once. Wherever God called us, we would go.

When our baby was eight months old, a call came from a thriving church in upstate New York, a thousand miles east of our home in Minneapolis. Penfield Presbyterian Church was located in a wealthy suburb of Rochester. I would be the associate pastor in charge of programs for children, youth, and families (which struck me as pretty much everyone). The executive presbyter told me that the position was a "plum." In fact, I would be the first female to serve this prestigious church. Doug and I were ecstatic and deeply grateful to God.

Still, we felt a sense of shock at how quickly the change would unfold and how complicated the logistics would be. We needed to sell our ramshackle house—an old Victorian that cost less than a BMW—and buy one in our new community. We quickly realized that housing prices in Penfield were completely out of our range. We would need two incomes, which meant finding a full-time job for Doug and full-time care for our two daughters.

The church's senior pastor, Reverend Zane Bolinger, phoned. Appearing to be helpful, he volunteered to plan my ordination service and the reception to follow. As he said, it was one chore he could take off my plate. Bolinger was a long-time pastor, beloved by his congregation. At sixty-two years old, he was twice my age and had recently been widowed. I felt honored that he offered to preach the ordination sermon. I knew that when I knelt for the moment of ordination, he would be the first to lay his hands on my head. I felt thrilled in anticipation of that holy moment.

I couldn't possibly have known that in a year's time Bolinger would lay his hands on me again, with unholy intentions.

THE TRAP IS LAID: TAMAR'S STORY

In 2 Samuel 13, the text uses the phrase "fell in love" to describe how Amnon lusted after his half-sister Tamar: "David's son Absalom had a beautiful sister whose name was Tamar; and David's son Amnon fell in love with her. Amnon was so tormented that he made himself ill because of his sister Tamar, for she was a virgin and it seemed impossible to Amnon to do anything to her" (2 Samuel 13:1-2).

Ancient texts use euphemisms too. Amnon "fell in love" and could not "do anything" to Tamar. But look! Help is on the horizon: "Amnon had a friend whose name was Jonadab, the son of David's brother Shimeah; and Jonadab was a very crafty man. He said to him, 'O son of the king, why are you so haggard morning after morning? Will you not tell me?'" (2 Samuel 13:3-4).

Can you hear cousin Jonadab's ingratiating tone? "O son of the king!" In other words, "O, you important man! You are not like other men!" Schemers have always orbited the powerful.

Whether they're tangential relatives, hangers-on, or opportunists, they know how to give influential men their heart's desire. Jonadab is the cunning type willing to offer up a woman's body to advance his own agenda.

The ruse that Jonadab concocts is wonderfully simple. Amnon could pretend to be sick. His appetite is gone, but it might be tempted with one of his sister's special recipes. Those steamed dumplings! Those are his favorite.

As Jonadab anticipated, David orders Tamar to Amnon's house to cook for him. Tamar cannot refuse the king's order, even if she suspects that she is being summoned to satisfy other appetites. Obediently, she prepares the dumplings and sets them before Amnon. He will not eat. He clears the room and orders Tamar to bring the food into his bedchamber. Is she wary about what will happen next? She does as she's told and the door closes behind her.

THE TRAP IS LAID: MY STORY

Before we moved, Doug was told he could secure a teaching job with his credentials, but he soon discovered that the local schools required a master's degree, which would require another full year of classes. After a long talk we decided it made sense for him to stay home and take care of our daughters full time, at least for this season. We would have to live off my salary, which was the minimum allowed by the denomination. We thought we could scrape by since we were used to living a simple student lifestyle.

I plunged into my work. My new boss, Bolinger, said we should get to know each other, especially since he would soon be preaching at my ordination service. He took me to lunch at his favorite restaurant. Over tempura and teriyaki he asked about the circumstances that led me to seminary. I told him my journey included a private trauma, and he assured me he would hold it in confidence. I trusted him. I also longed to move past the shame that shackled me. I wanted God to turn this trauma to good through my ministry.

So, I told him the story that I had rarely spoken about, which had been treated as unspeakable by my college and church culture. I explained that I'd been raped at gunpoint by intruders and that the ordeal had completely undone me—leaving me isolated, ashamed, and ruined. Everything certain in my life had dissolved in the space of hours. I told him these things because they were important pieces of my journey into ministry.

But the part Bolinger probed were the actual sexual assaults. He pressed me for details in a way that unsettled me, asking me questions even the detectives had not: what position did the rapist use, did he engage in "foreplay," had I been a virgin? Noting my discomfort, he reassured me that he was asking for my benefit, that he was an expert in pastoral counseling. He pressed on. Given my history, was it difficult for me to have intimate relationships with men now? I felt uneasy with the tenor of his questions but told myself that healing might entail discomfort. As he paid the bill, he said we should have lunch again the next day. The pattern of frequent lunches was set.

A few weeks later, Bolinger hatched a plan whereby we could become "copastors." That way I could take over as senior pastor when he retired in four years. Meanwhile, we could ask the church's governing board to make our salaries more level. The thought tantalized me. Honestly, why *were* our salaries so far apart? It was disheartening to work such long hours and be so completely broke.

Bolinger brought me a gift, a child-sized collectible plate and cup set. The china dishes had belonged to a very young child in the congregation who died tragically. After the funeral, the parents gave him the dishes as a keepsake, and now he bestowed them on me in the manner of Elijah casting his mantle over Elisha (see 1 Kings 19:19). I didn't see how I could refuse the gift, although I certainly didn't want the dishes. My healthy daughters weren't going to eat from them! And why would I want to be reminded of a tragic death that had nothing to do with me?

Another day he brought me a handmade heirloom quilt that had been in his family for more than a century. I still remember the heaviness of that quilt in my arms, the weight of thousands of stitches made by a faceless woman. I regretted ever making an offhand comment that I enjoyed pieced quilts. Another time he trundled a library cart containing some twenty-five volumes of Anchor Bible commentaries into my office. I knew I was supposed to be grateful for all his largesse, but I was frustrated. Nothing came of the pay raise he had dangled before me.

Meanwhile, I was swamped with responsibilities. The Sunday school boomed with nearly sixty children, and we also added a lively adult education program. I led or attended a meeting four or five nights a week. The teachers were responsive to my leadership. One remarked that the whole church had perked up on my arrival. She added, "And you've brought Zane [Bolinger] back to life."

My efforts in the programs for middle- and high-schoolers did not go as smoothly. The difficulties were not with the students but with the eight adult volunteers. Two of these were thirty-something men, recently divorced. One happened to be Bolinger's son; the other was his good friend. I felt that both men disliked me intensely from the get-go. They called me a "kill-joy" and seemed to take great delight in poking fun of my dilapidated car, complete with my daughters' car seats. What youth would want to ride with me when they could ride in these guys' hot cars?

The adult volunteers told me war stories about the glory days in the 1980s and about my predecessor, who played the guitar and had long hair "like Jesus." They said their planning meetings used to last until midnight. When I looked puzzled, someone explained that my predecessor confiscated people's watches so that no one knew how late it was getting to be.

That seemed unbelievable, so I asked the church secretary. She dropped her voice to say she heard some wild stories about those meetings, that they served alcohol and turned out the lights for "devotions." Her voice dropped even further. She heard people sometimes sat on each other's laps. We raised our eyebrows at each other and laughed nervously.

But maybe she misunderstood. Why would anyone turn a church meeting into a late night party? I certainly wanted to get the business done and go home to my family. Doug spent all day with two small children and no car. The least I could do was get home at a reasonable hour. I decided to ask Bolinger for advice. At our next lunch Bolinger presented me with jewelry that belonged to his late wife, accompanied by an emotional speech about how much I had come to mean to him in such a short time. I plunged ahead with my questions. Did previous youth planning meetings have a party atmosphere? Did they serve alcohol? He brushed my concerns aside. When a glass of dessert wine appeared before me, I could no longer deny what was happening. This behavior felt more like courtship than supervision.

Looking back, Bolinger's actions could be considered grooming behaviors. Whether he began his attentions with abuse in mind, I can't say. Certainly the behaviors spiraled. I do know that he attempted to forge an inappropriately intimate alliance by finding excuses to talk about sex on multiple occasions, beginning with my disclosure of my history of rape. At some point, I realized that his attitude toward the subject was lascivious.

When I realized that Bolinger's attentions were inappropriate, I told my husband that Bolinger had "fallen in love" with me. That phrase was the only way I could describe the dynamics. To say it aloud made me feel guilty, as if I had somehow led him on. The thought turned my stomach. This was 1991, before the language of sexual harassment became commonplace. I only knew that Bolinger sent out tentacles—inappropriate questions, ramped-up emotions, eagerness for attention—that entrapped me.

I felt like a hostage. Bolinger held power over me in every way. He was seasoned in ministry while I was inexperienced. He was financially secure while I was impoverished. He was well-connected in the denomination's regional networks while I was unknown. He was established at the church while I was brand new. He was the boss while I was the subordinate. He was male, and I was not.[4]

THE VIOLATION: TAMAR'S STORY

Tamar's ability to muster an argument while terrified and trapped in a bedchamber is stunning. She cries: "No, my brother, do not force me; for such a thing is not done in Israel; do not do anything so vile! As for me, where could I carry my shame? And as for you, you would be as one of the scoundrels in Israel. Now therefore, I beg you, speak to the king; for he will not withhold me from you" (2 Samuel 13:12-13). Tamar's suggestion may shock us since marriage to Amnon would be incestuous, but it was an option. Tamar is trying to protect her social self as well as her physical and sexual self. She knows her future depends on what Amnon does. If he marries her, she will have a place in the royal family. If he violates her, she will lose that place. Even a king's daughter can be ruined by what a man does to her.

But Amnon doesn't seem impressed with Tamar's ability to problem-solve while her very life is at stake. No, he is too "in love" to listen to the woman he supposedly loves. I'm grateful that Tamar's eloquent words became part of our canon, despite the fact that Amnon ignored them. We can herald Tamar as a woman of faith who pushed back against oppression, repression, and suppression. Scripture bears witness to her brave resistance, as well as the shame she bore unjustly.

Tamar was not only King David's beautiful daughter but also an intelligent person and gifted communicator. Despite all that—despite her fully exercising her moral agency within the limits of her power—she still became a pawn in a larger story about male desire and rivalry. Her *less-than* status set her up, creating the circumstances that victimized her, as detailed in 2 Samuel 13:14-15: "But [Amnon] would not listen to her; and being stronger than she, he forced her and lay with her. Then Amnon was seized with a very great loathing for her; indeed, his loathing was even greater than the lust he had felt for her. Amnon said to her, 'Get out!'"

THE VIOLATION: MY STORY

A little more than a year in, Bolinger physically assaulted me. I was working at my desk in my church office with my back to the door. Bolinger had just solved a problem and was elated with himself. He came into my office, spun my chair around to face him, put a hand on either side of my head, pulled me to him, and forcibly kissed my lips. In one reflexive motion, I said, "No," stood up, put my hands on his shoulders, and pushed him away.

When I shut the door behind him, I was trembling with fury and fear, physically overwhelmed by the realization of my vulnerability. I immediately drove home and told Doug what happened. He threatened to storm over and kneecap the man. Beet-red, he shouted that no man could assault his wife and get away with it. I had never seen my husband so upset. I couldn't imagine him hitting someone with a baseball bat. I was so afraid of losing my job that I found myself soothing him and wishing I had kept silent. When I returned to my office that afternoon—back to work!—a vase of purple irises crowned my desk and a note from Bolinger invited me out for dinner. I was flabbergasted and full of despair.

Bolinger and I did not have dinner. I don't believe we ever ate at the same table again (although we did preside over the Lord's Table together, a monthly tribulation). I did what I could to distance myself from him, such as turning my desk to face the door and keeping the door shut and locked. After a few days, I worked up my nerve and asked the church secretary to join me in Bolinger's office. I announced to both of them that I would never again be in a room alone with him. It was a rule. The secretary nodded and asked no questions.

The forcible kiss was, in one sense, only the culminating act in an escalating pattern of abuse. But that act changed everything. I couldn't continue to pretend, even to myself, that Bolinger was well-intentioned. I sought the help of a counselor who was an ordained pastor in another denomination. That I had to pay for these counseling sessions myself was salt in the wound. After I poured out my story, the counselor advised me to count the costs and stay silent. He reminded me, as if I didn't already know, that Bolinger held all the cards. Not only was he my boss and well-connected, he was beloved by the congregation.

Meanwhile, the October 1991 news cycle covered the confirmation hearings for Clarence Thomas, a nominee for the Supreme Court. Anita Hill, an attorney who had worked as an assistant to Thomas, testified that he had sexually harassed her.[5] I was riveted to the television. Hill's testimony was brave and eloquent. I didn't doubt that she spoke the truth and at great cost to herself. When the vote confirmed Thomas anyway, I was flattened. The deck was obviously stacked against a woman who spoke out against a powerful man, no matter how well she spoke. The abuser was rewarded while the woman was vilified.

I wanted to give up, move back to Minneapolis, and have a do-over. But I feared I would never get another position if I left this one so soon, under a shadow. Besides, I liked our little house—which we'd been able to afford because it stood along a minor highway. We had plans to fence the yard and turn the walk-out basement into a playroom. I longed to see our daughters playing there, safe and carefree. I wanted to provide stability for them and for Doug, who was such a trooper.

Beyond that, I was simply driven to succeed. And much about my ministry *was* successful.

I felt trapped, a maddening feeling. Even though I knew it was unfair, I lashed out at Doug. How in the world had I become the sole support of a family of four? It was an ugly time for our marriage as the desperation of the situation contaminated every interaction with guilt, blame, and frustration.

THE AFTERMATH: TAMAR'S STORY

What happens next is precisely what Tamar predicted would happen. Despite her pleas, Amnon casts her out of his bed-chamber:

> He called the young man who served him and said, "Put this woman out of my presence, and bolt the door after her." (Now she was wearing a long robe with sleeves; for this is how the virgin daughters of the king were clothed in earlier times.) So his servant put her out, and bolted the door after her. But Tamar put ashes on her head, and tore the long robe that she was wearing; she put her hand on her head, and went away, crying aloud as she went. (2 Samuel 13:17-19)

Tamar is grieving because she has lost her place within the royal family and society. Her full brother, Absalom, says, "'Has Amnon your brother been with you? Be quiet for now, my sister; he is your brother; do not take this to heart.' So Tamar remained, a desolate woman, in her brother Absalom's house" (2 Samuel 13:20). A traumatized Tamar is banished from the story even as her trauma provides the momentum to escalate events.

When King David hears about the assault he becomes angry, "but he would not punish his son Amnon, because he loved him, for he was his firstborn" (2 Samuel 13:21). Absalom, son number two, now has a perfect reason to hate his brother. The text doesn't say, but I speculate that Absalom's hatred for Amnon springs as much from his rivalrous desire to seize the throne as it does from his concern for his sister.

Maybe I'm wrong. Maybe Absalom really is terribly upset about what Amnon has done to Tamar. The fact is that, in 2 Samuel 13:20, he tells his sister, "Be quiet," and then in verse 28, he goes on to avenge her assault. Both extremes—shushing her and killing her rapist in bloody revenge—treat Tamar as having no agency. Why should Tamar vanish from the story that is ostensibly about her? Why should the two male characters drive all the action and make all the decisions? Each still holds power while Tamar does not.

Two years pass. Absalom throws a grand party, a sheep shearing feast so large that King David compels Amnon to attend with the other royals. This provides Absalom with an opportunity: "Then Absalom commanded his servants, 'Watch when Amnon's heart is merry with wine, and when I say to you, "Strike Amnon," then kill him. Do not be afraid; have I not myself commanded you? Be courageous and valiant'" (2 Samuel 13:28). The New American Bible translates that last sentence as "Be resolute and act manfully." Now that's a text to preach on, my friends! From a biblical viewpoint, what does it mean to "act manfully"? In this case, it means to commit murder for hire. Clearly, biblical gender roles can be problematic.

After the feast-turned-assassination, the other royals flee. A runner reports to David that all his sons have been killed. But

Jonadab, knowing the rivalry between the two brothers, suspects what really happened. He puts the best possible spin on
the situation, reminding David that it's likely not all his sons
are dead, just Amnon. And he's right.

As is true of epic tales, the story stretches on. King David
mourns for Amnon for three years, then forgives Absalom,
which cues the next round of manipulation. Absalom actively
tries to usurp his father's throne and battles David's army. This
doesn't end well either, with Absalom dangling by his hair
from the branches of an oak tree while an enemy runs three
spears through him. Still, when David mourns for Absalom, his
words capture the fullest expression of grief in all of Scripture:
"The king was deeply moved, and went up to the chamber over
the gate, and wept; and as he went, he said, 'O my son Absalom,
my son, my son Absalom! Would I had died instead of you, O
Absalom, my son, my son!'" (2 Samuel 18:33).

Note that in all these pages of Scripture, David mourns publicly for both Amnon and Absalom but not Tamar. In the
Hebrew Bible, daughters simply aren't worth grieving over.
Amnon raped David's daughter. Absalom actively tried to
usurp his throne. Yet both of these sons evoke tears and lamentation, while Tamar's fate bears no mention. Her obedience
netted her no reward. David's silence speaks volumes: Tamar's
life is not equal in value to those of her brothers. How painful
to be confronted with the sheer expendability of females in
Scripture—yet this is our religious heritage.

THE AFTERMATH: MY STORY

Looking back, I see that after Bolinger's assault I was trapped
by logistics, especially the need to earn a paycheck. But I can

also identify four beliefs that kept me captive. Some of these beliefs were accurate, and some false. I believed the following:

The church as an institution was a supreme value, and worthy.

My job as pastor was a vocation to which God had called me.

I should be grateful for my place as a token woman in a patriarchal system.

As a previous victim, I had decreased worth.

Even the beliefs that *were* true—the first two—did not serve me well. The church might be worthy, and the job of pastor might be a calling from God, but these beliefs are easily twisted. Since Jesus' life and work was a willing sacrifice, Christian organizations tend to enshrine self-sacrifice as noble. This handily exploits their pastors' tendencies to overwork. But no pastor is called to sacrifice her life, or her family's life, for the sake of a congregation's dysfunction.

The dynamics around noble self-sacrifice only intensify when the pastor is female. The church, like the larger culture, devalues the work of women. Since I was the first female clergy at Penfield Presbyterian, there's no doubt that gender issues complicated people's expectations of me and their evaluation of my efforts.

Statements three and four are overtly false beliefs. The idea that women have less value than men and should therefore be grateful for a token place is the very definition of a sexist system. But women are not immune from sexist beliefs. I was raised with these beliefs and unconsciously allowed them to color my world for decades. What's more, enduring rape at gunpoint added a heaping helping of shame on me.

It wasn't until I spent years writing my memoir that I fully unpacked my feelings and beliefs about gender. Not all beliefs are readily apparent or logical. Despite my deep conviction that I was a beloved child of God, for years I struggled with feeling *less than*. This is why it's important to unearth the hidden beliefs that drive us, both as individual believers and as communities of faith.

Theologies are always shored up by two simple words: *Scripture says!* Scripture says many things, including many contradictory things. When we construct our beliefs, we must take into account the entire arc of Scripture. We must be aware of the temptation to "baptize" what feels good and right because it's known and comfortable. To many people, the male attachment to power seems natural and normal. It's not difficult to find Scripture passages that support lopsided ideas about the genders. But we must remember that Scripture exists within a cultural context. Haven't we just read Absalom's exhortation to his servants to "act manfully!" and plunge a spear into the next king of Israel? We have also heard Tamar's reverberating plea to her brothers, "Where can I carry my shame?" How we interpret these lines of dialogue will shape our church's culture.

THE TEXT ASKS US

1. Where should Tamar have carried her shame, and by what means?

2. What does it mean to "act manfully"?

MY HOPE

My hope is that the church will hear Tamar's question, "Where can I carry my shame?" and answer, to the church. Churches can welcome victims and survivors, hear their stories, and heal their wounds. Churches can protect the vulnerable, challenge and prosecute abusers, and become a space that is both safer and braver.

CHAPTER TWO

SILENCE AND SHAME

You tell me it gets better, it gets better in time
You say I'll pull myself together
Pull it together, you'll be fine
Tell me, what the hell do you know

LADY GAGA, "TIL IT HAPPENS TO YOU"

[Jesus] said to her, "Daughter, your faith has made you
well; go in peace, and be healed of your disease."

MARK 5:34

ABOUT A YEAR AFTER Reverend Zane Bolinger physically assaulted me in my office at Penfield Presbyterian Church (PPC), I resolved to bring the matter to the church leaders. Despite my counselor's advice to count the costs and stay silent, I knew I needed to tell my story and seek redress. Costs can be counted in all sorts of ways. I'd been working hard. I deserved to be heard.

My counselor reluctantly suggested that if I *insisted* on telling, the appropriate body to tell would be the personnel committee of the church, which had not met in many years. I called a meeting.

The chair of the committee, who I'll call Rodney, was Bolinger's best friend and golf buddy. I had never spoken to him as he was a senior citizen, the only demographic not included in my job description. Two of the other committee members were men who served as elders on the church's governing board. They both held middle management jobs at Kodak, the largest employer in the region.

The fourth member, who I'll call Cindy, was a psychologist. Cindy had been assigned to be my mentor when I first arrived at PPC. We met once to discuss my spiritual journey, and I told her many of the same things I told Bolinger: that I'd grown up in a conservative churchgoing home and learned to be a "good girl" and that after I was raped at gunpoint in college I had a crisis of faith that eventually landed me in seminary. At our meeting, Cindy and I discussed the dark night of the soul and the meaning of redemption.

We met one more time that I remember, for breakfast. Cindy urged me to practice self-care by attending Rochester's cultural events—why didn't Doug and I join the symphony? I thought, *Maybe because we can't afford McDonald's without coupons?*

When the breakfast check came, I bristled at having to expend precious funds to pay for a meal I hadn't enjoyed to hear advice I couldn't use from a woman who was supposed to help me—all while sticking my husband with the entire morning routine at home. The final insult came when the symphony people called our home . . . at supper time . . . repeatedly. Cindy had given them our number.

I want to be fair, because Cindy tried. She had my family over for supper once, a fun evening where she pulled out old Barbie dolls to entertain the girls. She generously lent us the use of her second home in the Finger Lakes. But sometimes, despite their best efforts, people are unable to offer meaningful help. Had I been honest about our finances, perhaps she would have gone to bat for a wage increase. After all, the *church* should have felt ashamed for how little they paid me. But I thought the situation was all my fault—me and my dreams of ordination and my talk about God's call to ministry. Now Doug's career was on hold, and I couldn't provide for the family. My feelings of anger, fear, guilt, and recrimination were as familiar as my pillow. They added up to shame.

TWO DAUGHTERS AND JESUS (MARK 5:21-43)

Healing is a universal need. When we talk about the human condition, we're talking about frailty and brokenness. All of us need healing of some sort. Although I have yet to experience sustained physical illness, I have often been soul-sick. My need for healing from shame is why I particularly love the story of Jesus healing two daughters.

Jesus has just crossed Lake Galilee by boat and is walking through a little town on the western shore. An important man named Jairus, a synagogue leader, rushes up to Jesus "and begged him repeatedly, 'My little daughter is at the point of death. Come and lay your hands on her, so that she may be made well, and live'" (Mark 5:23).

A later verse states that the daughter is twelve years old, so "little daughter" may be an expression of affection rather than information about her age. We know that she is beloved by her father, who prostrates himself before Jesus. Prostration can be a sign of exhaustion and despair, but it can also be a gesture of reverence, submission, and trust. Jairus has doubtless heard that others were healed when Jesus laid hands on them. He expresses a confident trust that Jesus can do the same for his daughter.

Jesus agrees to help. Together they head toward Jairus's un-named village. The text says, "And a large crowd followed him and pressed in on him" (Mark 5:24). That Greek verb (*syneth-libon*) is sometimes translated as *thronged, pressed on all sides,* or *compressed.* It could be translated literally as the crowd *gathered on top of him.* This is the Jesus-Amoeba in action, under pressure. At this moment a second daughter appears, although she's not yet called "daughter." She is simply an unnamed woman: "Now there was a woman who had been suffering from hemorrhages for twelve years" (Mark 5:25).

Since we can't name her according to male family members (like the daughter of Jairus), tradition names her by disease. Have you ever noticed that biblical scholars seem to co-opt the speech of medical students when they identify biblical characters? This hemorrhaging daughter is often called *The Woman with the Issue of Blood.* Before her came *The Demoniac* and before him *The Leper, The Paralytic,* and *The Man with the Withered Hand.* The names are helpful, of course, providing titles for each story. But we should beware the dynamic of healthy people labeling sick ones. We should notice how this distances us from the action of the story. *We* are not hemorrhaging, or blind, or paralyzed, or possessed by demons. We are healthy people reading about sick ones, and healthy people don't generally seek a cure. But who is healthy, and who is sick? Our delusions of health—our attachment to the temporary condition of being able-bodied—may prevent us from entering the gospel in the appropriate way.

The woman with the issue of blood knows she is sick. She's been bleeding for twelve years, the same number of years Jairus's daughter has been alive. The symmetry between these two daughters and their dozen years invites comparisons.

Jesus is engulfed by the crowd as the bleeding woman approaches. Undaunted, she worms her way from the edge toward the center, stretching her arm toward the source of healing. When I was a child, I loved picturing this. The scene was hazy but dramatic: the surging crowd, the woman with her arm outstretched, her blood *issuing*.

Issuing from where? No one ever said. Like most children, I was impressed with blood, especially my own. While the preacher talked, I invented elaborate accident scenarios. Maybe she skidded on gravel and scraped her knee. Maybe her big brother knocked her down and her bone was poking out. Whatever made her blood *issue*, it wouldn't stop.

THE PERSONNEL COMMITTEE MEETING: MY STORY

My counselor helped me prepare for the meeting with the church's personnel committee. I didn't expect to receive overwhelming support, but I assumed I would get a fair hearing. I showed up that evening with my notes in hand. To my surprise, Bolinger occupied a seat at the table. The committee chair, Rodney (Bolinger's best friend), said he had a right to be there. I said I would prefer that he left. None of the other three committee members could understand why I would want to exclude him, so he remained.

With Bolinger sitting right there, I pressed forward with my agenda. I told the committee that ever since I began my work, Bolinger had behaved in ways that were inappropriate and overly familiar. As examples, I cited the restaurant lunches and gift-giving. I mentioned the gift of jewelry belonging to his late wife and the strawberries he hand-dipped in chocolate.

With a dismissive laugh, Rodney said he would gladly take my problems—someone showering him with expensive meals and gifts! I said that Bolinger's courtship behavior had escalated to the point of him assaulting me in my office.

With an eager smile, Bolinger leaned forward in his chair. He acknowledged that he had kissed me. He said it was normal to express affection with a kiss.

I countered, saying it was a kiss on the mouth, not the cheek, and had been forced on me. I felt so repulsed that I found it difficult to sit in the same room and talk about this.

Rodney said I misunderstood the situation and that Bolinger felt "pure Christian love" for me.

I retorted that those words were inaccurate. My anger and frustration leaked out in tears. Around the room the other members murmured, *so sorry that you're upset.*

At this point, Cindy, the therapist and my assigned mentor— and the only other woman in the room—chimed in. In a burst of feeling, she said that I was probably extra-sensitive to the situation because of my sexual history. All eyes turned on me. Cindy explained that I had endured a previous sexual trauma, which explained my tears now. As a victim, she said, I was "uniquely vulnerable."

I was shocked that she had broken my confidence. My tears intensified, and I was unable to speak. Score another point for Bolinger. That Ruth was certainly an emotional mess.

CONSIDERING LEVITICUS

When I was in my early twenties, I heard a sermon that changed my life. It was preached by Reverend Julie Neraas, the first woman I ever heard preach. Without embarrassment, Neraas explained that the woman's *issue of blood* was a menstrual irregularity. In other words, this woman's monthly flow never stopped. She had a period that never ended. To post-modern ears, all that bleeding may sound miserable and highly inconvenient. But it was much worse than that. In the absence of medical care, her condition may well have been life-threatening. It was also a severe social handicap. At the time, menstruating women were considered ritually unclean. The Levitical law is quite specific:

> When a woman has a discharge of blood, the impurity of her menstrual period lasts seven days. Anyone who touches her is unclean until evening. Everything on which she lies or sits during her period is unclean. Anyone who touches her bed or anything on which she sits must wash his clothes and bathe in water; he remains unclean until evening.
>
> If a man sleeps with her and her menstrual blood gets on him, he is unclean for seven days and every bed on which he lies becomes unclean.
>
> If a woman has a discharge of blood for many days, but not at the time of her monthly period, or has a discharge that continues beyond the time of her period, she is unclean the same as during the time of her period. Every bed on which she lies during the time of the discharge and everything on which she sits becomes unclean the same as in her monthly period. Anyone who touches these things becomes unclean and must wash his clothes and bathe in water; he remains unclean until evening.
>
> When she is cleansed from her discharge, she is to count off seven days; then she is clean. On the eighth day she is to take two doves or two pigeons and bring them to the priest at the entrance to the Tent of Meeting. The priest will offer one for an Absolution-Offering and the other for a Whole-Burnt-Offering. The priest will make atonement for her in the presence of GOD because of the

discharge that made her unclean. (Leviticus 15:19-30, *The Message*, paraphrase)

The sheer length of the regulations is impressive. That the law reaches into the most private areas of life, dictating so much female labor, is also worth noting.

The bleeding woman is not just inconvenienced but nearly disabled by her unending menstrual flow. If she follows the letter of the law, she must live alone, which the text suggests is the case, as no family members are mentioned.

A significant question underlying the text is to what degree the Levitical law was observed in small towns in Palestine during the first century. Dr. Amy-Jill Levine, a Jewish scholar of the New Testament, asserts that the law was not observed in towns without a synagogue, on the grounds that the people wouldn't have been able to make the required sacrifices, due to travel time.[1] In that case, the town's location (and therefore the distance to a synagogue) is a crucial, but unknown, fact. That Jairus, a synagogue leader, has traveled to reach Jesus raises, but does not answer, that question. His presence as a rabbinic authority adds tension to the text in another way as well. The bleeding woman is alerted to possible repercussions if she violates the law.

In her book *The Misunderstood Jew*, Levine argues that because the text doesn't specifically cite the Levitical laws, they were irrelevant.[2] If this were true, it would significantly change my understanding of this text. However, most Christian scholars assume that the law undergirded Jewish existence in first century Palestine. Certainly, Jesus was well-versed in the law—their application was frequently at issue.[3]

Among the information we're given about the bleeding woman's circumstances is something unusual—a line of internal dialogue: "She had heard about Jesus, and came up behind him in the crowd and touched his cloak, *for she said*, 'If I but touch his clothes, I will be made well'" (Mark 5:27-28, emphasis mine). A number of translations alter the text to specify, "for she said *to herself.*" In other words, she wouldn't have spoken aloud because her intended actions were technically illegal. Whether she whispered or thought them, these words make palpable her need for healing, her hope, and her fear.

The bleeding woman commits a desperate act, and it's easy to see why. In a time and place where women have very specific roles, she is unable to fill them. A woman is expected to bear children, but she is unable to conceive.[4] A woman is expected to put dinner on the table, but she cannot do the marketing and food preparation if she is ritually impure. If she's unable to do these ordinary tasks, what is she good for?

That question isn't rhetorical. It has an answer: she is literally good for nothing. In an economic sense, she is worthless.

Since the woman has been in this condition for twelve years, we can assume that any husband is long gone. It was easy for men to divorce women. And who would blame a man for divorcing a worthless woman? No wonder she spent "all that she had" on doctors (Mark 5:26). They are her only hope.

How did she support herself those twelve years? If you've ever been seriously ill, you may identify with the economic equation of this story. The woman "was no better, but rather grew worse" (Mark 5:26). Her situation drained her financially and physically, leaving her both destitute and anemic.

As I listened to Neraas's sermon, I saw myself in the bleeding woman. This was no skinned knee oozing blood. This was a desperate woman who knew she had little value, transformed because she reached out to touch Jesus' robe. For the first time, I grasped the enormity of her courage and the miraculous power that healed her. I saw her as an agent in her own life, making a daring and risky choice. And I saw her as completely dependent on Jesus, determined to worm her way to him, even if that meant taking her life in her hands.

"PURE CHRISTIAN LOVE": MY STORY

At the personnel committee meeting, Rodney said that Bolinger felt "pure Christian love" for me. Words matter to me, so I've thought a lot about those three, which sounded so unassailable yet papered over sexual misconduct.

Instead of giving credence to my experience of assault, the personnel committee decided that Bolinger's *intentions* were the axis on which their decision would turn. While it's always dangerous to ascribe motives to someone else, they were quick to pinpoint Bolinger's. And could you invent a more righteous motive than *pure Christian love*? Also highly convenient. This motive took Bolinger off the hook. What's more, the personnel committee was off the hook; there was no need to challenge the person in power. No need to enforce accountability. No need to raise an issue like consent. No need to even ask follow-up questions.

If his behavior was *pure* and *Christian* and *loving*, my protest was unfounded. They could close their ears to me and feel virtuous about doing so. In fact, my complaint—and my angry tears—suggested that I was the impure, un-Christian, unloving one.

Out of the three words, the one that bothered me most was *Christian*. It pinned Bolinger's misdeeds onto Jesus' apron strings. How do you think Jesus feels about that? It's one thing to say he washes away our sin. It's another to expect him to clean up a mess we won't even look at, much less admit we made. How do people dare treat the Son of God like a housekeeper in a low-rent motel? Is it his job to clean up the empty beer cans and vomit so that we can pretend the blow out never happened?

I don't remember how that meeting ended, but in my imagination, there was a thwack—the clap on the back, the ranks closing, the Good Ol' Boys (and their female ally) shutting the clubhouse doors. A forcible kiss wasn't enough to disturb business as usual.

THE SO-CALLED APOLOGIES OF POWERFUL MEN

When Aretha Franklin, the Queen of Soul, died in August 2018, her funeral service was eight hours of live music. Among the performers was Ariana Grande, a twenty-five-year-old singer who delivered a pitch-perfect version of Aretha's hit "(You Make Me Feel Like) A Natural Woman." Bishop Charles Ellis, who was officiating, pulled the singer to the podium. With his arm clamped around Grande's torso and his hand visibly pressing against the side of her right breast, he made a jokey, belittling comment about her name, comparing it to a Taco Bell menu item.

Since the service was televised, social media was quick to spread the pictures that held up a mirror to Ellis's groping hand. The bishop made a blithe apology that put the blame on God: "It would never be my intention to touch any woman's breast. I don't know, I guess I put my arm around her. Maybe I crossed the border. Maybe I was too friendly or familiar but again, I apologize. I hug all the female and male artists. Everybody that was up, I shook their hands and hugged them. That's what we are all about in the church. We are all about love."[5]

For me, watching that so-called apology felt like a flashback. A powerful man groped an attractive, younger woman, then justified his actions by talking about the love of God, as if God were responsible for his lack of boundaries. I was grateful for the social media response that called Ellis to account, even if it couldn't force him to examine his own heart.

A helpful way to describe this dynamic is the concept of *male fragility*. Both Bolinger and Ellis held powerful positions that gave them access to younger women, which they exploited. But when confronted with their actions each reacted as if he were the victim rather than the victimizer.

There's a parallel idea when discussing racism called *white fragility*. This describes the reaction of white people who refuse to admit they harbor racist attitudes or benefit from racist systems. Both kinds of *fragility* use feigned shock as an excuse to avoid the hard work of doing justice—which begins with self examination and moves out to confront an unjust system. Both terms identify and describe a certain moral laziness.

It hurts to acknowledge that the world is not fair, that systems of oppression exist, that we've profited from someone else's pain. To admit that our society is not a level playing field may mean giving up power and privilege we unwittingly enjoy. *Fragility* refers to those who will admit that inequality exists only if they are seen as one of the exceptions, one of the "good ones." See how seductive this perspective is? After all, we know we're not bad people with evil intentions. This is the nut of the reason that the movement for racial justice faces so many obstacles. Individuals who intend no evil refuse to acknowledge that they participate in and benefit from unjust systems.

The same is true for gender justice. Men who are accustomed to having power and privilege often refuse to acknowledge the advantages they enjoy. They remain willfully blind to the patriarchal laws and norms that make their lives easier and more profitable. When they do display sexist behaviors, they minimize them, if only because these behaviors seem normal. Underlying such behaviors is the assumption that women are less important than they themselves. When called to account, they protest that they are by no means sexist: *I'm one of the good ones. The victim of a misunderstanding. Let me explain.*

Church culture adds a component of pious talk that is especially damaging to people of faith. Both Bolinger and Ellis excused their abusive behavior with talk about God's love. To overlay abuse with God-talk is to layer further abuse on the victim. Sanctioning injustice with the "love of God" is a double whammy for victims but occurs frequently in church circles. I'd love to hear how Jesus would respond.

HEALING: THE BLEEDING WOMAN

The bleeding woman grasps the bottom edge of Jesus' robe and immediately feels a shock. Healing courses through her body like voltage.

Jesus is being pressed by the crowd, jostled about by human contact. But this is no ordinary touch: "Immediately aware that power had gone forth from him, Jesus turned about in the crowd and said, 'Who touched my clothes?'" (Mark 5:30). Perhaps it cost Jesus something to heal a sick person, so he wanted to look the individual in the eye. The disciples intervene.

They often have to manage these things for Jesus, God love him. Jesus is terrible at logistics, always slowing down, always getting sidetracked. And the crowd! Look at it. Constantly growing. How could anyone possibly know who touched him?

But Jesus knows what happened. What's more, he knows the risk the woman took. Yet he persists in asking: Who touched me? In effect, Jesus asks her to risk her life by admitting what she has done.

The next moment astonishes me. Why doesn't she slip away? She's cured and doesn't need anything more from Jesus. Admitting her actions can only cause trouble with the authorities. Still, she doesn't run. "But the woman, knowing what had happened to her, came in fear and trembling, fell down before him, and told him the whole truth" (Mark 5:33).

And what does Jesus say? To this bleeding woman, this law-breaker, this good for nothing woman? He calls her, "Daughter" (Mark 5:34). This woman who had no one, and nothing, now belongs to Jesus. She is his kin.

In that single word, *daughter*, Jesus claims *all* of us as daughters. Every broken, bleeding one of us. Every law-breaking one of us. We are *all* called daughters of Jesus. He's using the word in its generic sense, so men are included. Jesus calls them *daughter*. The word is sweet; since I'm a daughter, and the mother of daughters, the word is like honey in my mouth. But it's also a powerful word, a belonging word.

HEALING: MY STORY

When I heard that life-changing sermon about the bleeding woman, I was in my mid-twenties. Five years had passed since I'd been held at gunpoint and raped. Much private prayer had repaired my faith, and I was grateful for that healing. But I was seeking a faith community where people of different races worshiped together and women had value. I was still recovering from shame.

Decades later, Elizabeth Smart put words to my feelings. She was abducted from her home at age fourteen and held captive and raped daily for nine months. When she described her highly publicized ordeal, she said the shame of rape made her feel like used chewing gum. Worthless. Used up. She feared that her Mormon culture, which highly valued sexual purity, would not welcome her home.[6] I don't mean to compare our stories in scale, but I resonated with her words. I knew how it felt to be treated as *less than*, first by the rapists and then on my Christian campus, with a scarlet blazon on my chest.

Hearing that transformative sermon in the presence of sisters and brothers—strangers to me at the time—made me feel profoundly welcomed. I was not alone anymore. In the midst of the crowd, Jesus saw me, as ruined as I felt, and called me daughter.

TEMPTATIONS FOR CHURCHES: MY STORY

Once Bolinger's behavior, including the forcible kiss, was excused as "pure Christian love," Rodney asked, "What can we do to make this go away?" The question surprised me at the time because it was a tacit admission of guilt. If there *was* no problem, as he had just asserted, why would it need to "go away"? I didn't understand that powerful persons can make unpleasant things disappear. I had experienced the opposite truth—that trauma never disappears.

I was naive, with a childlike trust in these leaders. Presbyterians call their leaders *elders* to refer to their role, not their age.

But at the time I was decades younger than the elders. I believed they would be insightful, discerning, and courageous. Once they understood the problem, they would want to fix it, and would know how.

I didn't understand a church's tremendous pull toward institutional self-preservation. I also didn't realize that churchgoers who love a pastor feel pulled to protect him (or her), even when they know the pastor is wrong. And I certainly didn't understand how easy it is to *not know* something inconvenient.

Another factor I underestimated was the intricate web of relationships within the church. Each person affected so many others. For instance, Bolinger's son—who I felt disliked me—was in a position to influence many in ways I could not see. And if he didn't like me *before* the personnel committee meeting, can you imagine how he felt *after* I confronted his "dear old dad"?

Truth telling is hard work. It exposes ugliness. In contrast, respectability has a smooth and pleasing veneer. No wonder good Christian people are tempted to turn a blind eye in the name of Jesus. It is easier to dismiss the abused than to confront the abuser, especially one who is beloved.

Two groundbreaking authors in the field of church response to sexual abuse are Marie Fortune and James Poling. They call for "a courageous and assertive response on the part of the church to abusers in its midst," a position that contrasts sharply with church leaders who tolerate the perpetrator out of a "mistaken understanding of God's love for all people."[7] According to Fortune and Poling, misguided tolerance is the result of yielding to six temptations:

⁊ The temptation of disbelief.

⁊ The temptation to protect the church's image.

\# The temptation to blame the victim.

\# The temptation to sympathize with the abuser.

\# The temptation to protect the abuser from the consequences of their behavior.

\# The temptation of cheap grace.

Penfield Presbyterian Church succumbed to each of these
six temptations. The leaders disbelieved that Bolinger was
abusive. They tried to silence my voice to protect the church's
image. They blamed me, tearful Ruth, who was conveniently a
prior victim and therefore suspect. They sympathized with
Bolinger's attempts to "lovingly" supervise me. Instead of
holding him accountable, they protected him from the consequences of his behavior. They then whitewashed the whole
thing with "pure Christian love," which is the very definition
of cheap grace. These actions were not just a failure to respond
to the initial abuse but an active layering of further abuse.

This often happens in faith communities unless people learn
to push past simplistic notions of grace and redemption. As
Judith Herman points out in her landmark book about treating
people who have experienced clinical trauma, avoidance is the
most common response to abuse:

> It is very tempting to take the side of the perpetrator. All
> the perpetrator asks is that the bystander do nothing. He
> appeals to the universal desire to see, hear, and speak no
> evil. The victim, on the contrary, asks the bystander to
> share the burden of pain. The victim demands action, en-
> gagement, and remembering.[8]

Did the volunteer members of the personnel committee
sign up for heavy lifting? People who agree to serve on a church

committee aren't necessarily prepared to deal with issues such as sexual harassment and abuse. It's not surprising that they falter and fail. While very few believers set out to intentionally harm their church, pastor, or vulnerable persons, they come with assumptions that can do harm. We need to recognize and confront such assumptions in ourselves and others.

HEALING: JAIRUS'S DAUGHTER

After Jesus heals the bleeding woman, the twelve-year-old daughter of Jairus is still waiting. A messenger arrives to tell Jairus that his daughter has died. "But overhearing what they said, Jesus said to the leader of the synagogue, 'Do not fear, only believe'" (Mark 5:36).

The word translated as *overhearing* might also be translated as *ignoring*. The world that Jesus operates within is different from the ordinary world, so he ignores what seems to be real. In this other reality, the girl is only sleeping. When Jesus goes to the house where people are mourning, crying, and wailing, he says, "'Why do you make a commotion and weep? The child is not dead but sleeping.' And they laughed at him. Then he put them all outside, and took the child's father and mother and those who were with him, and went in where the child was" (Mark 5:39-40).

The mourners (who might include paid mourners) laugh at Jesus, so he sends them outside. In Jesus' world, those who don't believe are put outside while those who believe get to stay. Then Jesus takes the child's parents and Peter, James, and John into the child's bedchamber.

He took her by the hand and said to her, "Talitha cum," which means, "Little girl, get up!" And immediately the girl got up and began to walk about (she was twelve years of age). At this they were overcome with amazement. He strictly ordered them that no one should know this, and told them to give her something to eat. (Mark 5:41-43)

Jesus initiated this healing through the laying on of hands, a fact worth noting. The simplest of all forms of human contact restores life. The text ends with a lovely postscript, a sort of denouement, as Jesus tells them to "give her something to eat" (Mark 5:43). Commentaries point out that after a resurrection or resuscitation, Scripture often records that the person eats food, a form of proof that the once-dead person is really alive again. After all, dead people don't eat.

But I think the commentators miss another point. Jesus is reminding the stunned parents, *your twelve-year-old daughter just traveled through the portals of death and back. She probably needs a snack.* Jesus cares about our bodily lives, even female bodies. It doesn't matter whether we're on the cusp of puberty, such as Jairus's daughter, or long past childbearing age, such as the bleeding woman. Each female is claimed by Jesus as a *daughter* worth healing.

What a powerful text for survivors of sexual assault. As we embrace our own daughterhood—and each other's daughterhood—we form a sisterhood, powerful in solidarity. Through the enduring power of the gospel, Jesus continues to raise up daughters who will fight together until all are heard, seen, and empowered to health and wholeness.

TO BE CONTINUED: MY STORY

It may not surprise you that the problems at PPC did *not* "go away." Eventually I knew that I would have to "go away." As thrilled as I'd been to be ordained to my first ministry position, I felt even happier to leave it. I still loved God, and I still loved the idea of church. I loved many of the people at PPC. Pastoral work is soul work, connecting on a deep level. But after two years, I knew it was time to look for another call. Bolinger had retired (ahead of schedule), but the problems did not retire with him. I thought of it as rot at the core of the system, surfacing in various ways—the sexual harassment, the lack of respect given to me as pastor, and the poor boundaries of the adult volunteers in the youth program. I could not fix these things. I hated to think that another female clergy might fill my position and face the same struggles, but at least Bolinger was out of the picture.

It took another year to find a position and relocate my family. In 1993, I accepted a call to become the solo pastor of a small rural church in Illinois. Before we moved, Doug and I seriously considered whether or not to bring an accusation against Bolinger through the Presbyterian courts. I wanted to model to our young daughters that women should push back against mistreatment. But I feared what it would cost our family in terms of time, energy, and negative emotion. I'd been through a court process before, when I testified against one of the rapists in 1978. As powerful and positive as that had been, I knew how to count the costs of court appearances and their inevitable delays. I also understood the power dynamics that prevented the PPC personnel committee from hearing me. If similar dynamics were at play in the regional church—and why wouldn't they be?—my story would only go unheard again.

After weighing the possibility of legal action, we dropped the idea. Instead, we "shook the dust off our sandals" as we left that contentious place (see Mark 6:11). I consoled myself that we still had everything that mattered. Doug and I funneled our energies into our marriage, daughters, and careers.

Doug found a teaching job while I learned to thrive in ministry to a small, rural church. The white clapboard building was postcard-pretty, and much about our new life was idyllic. When I could make the time, I even worked on writing a novel about a clergywoman serving a small, rural church in an idyllic setting. The drama was supplied by a lurking colleague modeled on Bolinger. In that space, if not elsewhere, I was the one with authority, the author. I controlled what happened to the characters. It would be many years before I would tell my story again to church authorities.

THE TEXTS ASKS US

1. Will we notice and heal the bleeding ones among us?

2. Will we restore to life those who are apparently dead?

MY HOPE

My hope is that churches will dare to break the silence and shame around women's bleeding bodies and tap the healing power in Jesus' garment.

CHAPTER THREE

THE SYSTEM AND SECRECY

If you want to keep a secret you must also hide it from yourself.

GEORGE ORWELL

Now you are the body of Christ and individually members of it.

1 CORINTHIANS 12:27

IN 1999, SIX YEARS AFTER I LEFT my position at Penfield Presbyterian Church (PPC), I received a phone call from a pastor in Rochester I'll call John, who I once met briefly. He told me he was consulting with PPC because of "problems." John's voice put air quotes around the word. Someone told him I had had similar "problems." Would I be willing to tell him what happened? I asked John what he intended to do with the information, and he gave a vague answer. I suspected—hoped—that someone might be bringing charges against my former boss, Zane Bolinger, so I told John I'd speak with him.

For almost an hour, I answered his questions about my tenure at PPC. I got out old calendars to give facts and dates. Then I again asked John about the nature of the current "problems." He hedged. I pressed. Finally I asked if any charges had been filed. John said something like "depends what kind of charges you mean." I felt momentarily elated that someone might be charging Bolinger. But what John said next shocked me. Someone else at PPC had been charged with abusing a child.

My legs gave way and I dropped to the floor. I wanted to expose secrets but not this. Dear God, not a child.

John wouldn't volunteer anything more, but I peppered him with questions and wormed out a few facts. The abuser was not the pastor . . . a long-time member . . . a volunteer leader . . . in the youth program . . . for many years.

I immediately knew who it was. "If you won't tell me, I'll tell you!" I shouted the man's name. "I was keeping my eye on him! Always cozying up to the senior high girls. Once I saw him kiss a girl!" I was worked up, my sense of alarm triggered once again. "I told one of the other leaders but she scoffed—"

John cut me off. "That's not the guy."

I pressed my case with more details.

"Ruth, that's not him. This guy abused a boy. A pre-adolescent boy."

After I hung up, I sat on the floor a long time. I was completely humbled by what I missed—what someone suffered on my watch. Eventually I heard the door slam; one of my daughters was home from school. My precious pre-adolescent girl.

THE APOSTLE PAUL ON ONE BODY

Ever since the apostle Paul wrote a letter to the church at Corinth, the Christian church has understood itself to be one body with many members. This organic image means that faith is not a matter of individual belief practiced alone but a shared experience. Our belief connects us to other believers. Together, we form a living organism called the body of Christ. Paul describes it this way: "For just as the body is one and has many members, and all the members of the body, though many, are one body, so it is with Christ" (1 Corinthians 12:12). Those who love and follow Jesus comprise that body. Each person is a member, or a limb.

During the time of Paul's writings, the metaphor of a body was commonly used within the Roman world to describe political entities. The image reinforced the logic of hierarchy within "the body politic." When a group of people form a body it makes sense that the head should be in charge while the hands and feet should do the dirty work.

In contrast, Paul uses the image to exult in the variety of the body's members with their individual functions and their organic unity:

> But as it is, God arranged the members in the body, each one of them, as he chose. If all were a single member, where would the body be? As it is, there are many members, yet one body. The eye cannot say to the hand, "I have no need of you," nor again the head to the feet, "I have no need of you." (1 Corinthians 12:18-21)

Paul holds up a model of interdependence. He goes on to laud the body's weaker, less respectable, and inferior members. Not only are these members as valuable as the head, they are given greater honor. The vision is one of equality and mutuality.

> On the contrary, the members of the body that seem to be *weaker* are indispensable, and those members of the body that we think less honorable we clothe with greater honor, and our *less respectable* members are treated with greater respect; whereas our more respectable members

do not need this. But God has so arranged the body, giving the greater honor to the *inferior* member, that there may be no dissension within the body, but the members may have the same care for one another. (1 Corinthians 12:22-25, emphasis added)

The words *weaker*, *less respectable*, and *inferior* most likely refer to the social and economic dimensions of life—in other words, to status. In the body of Christ, the members of low status have as much worth and value as the members of high status. Paul's teaching is radical. The lowly are equal to the powerful. The commanding head is no better than the dirty-working hands, the dust-covered feet. Imagine how incoherent and pointless—if not threatening—Paul's model must have appeared to minds calibrated to hierarchy.

The parts of the body even rely on each other to manage their emotional lives, their suffering and rejoicing: "If one member suffers, all suffer together with it; if one member is honored, all rejoice together with it" (1 Corinthians 12:26). Suffering and rejoicing belong to every member of the body, and the whole body. This is wholly different from the top-down Roman world where the only member whose feelings mattered was the member at the top.

Paul's language about *suffering* also addresses the more sobering implications of being a body, that a body is liable to get sick, and when it does, every part will suffer. We know this to be true in our own physicality. Infection can spread. Pain can shoot from a joint through a whole limb. Physical distress can lead to psychological distress, and vice versa. These common experiences may be the reason our society opts for medical models in talking about evil. We call evil a *cancer*. We refer to evildoers as *sick* individuals. These analogies offer an explanation —too often a facile one that prevents deeper exploration. Paul's metaphor invites us to look more closely at the body's vulnerability, including the mechanisms by which sickness invades. Who, exactly, are the *weaker* members who deserve compassion and mercy? How should the body react when its more powerful members cause harm?

A VICTIM COMES FORWARD

In January of 1997, three former members of PPC—a twenty-one-year old man and his parents—visited the new senior pastor, who I'll call Reverend Mayberry. The family had a horrifying story to tell. The young man had been sexually abused at the church over a period of three years in the early 1980s, from ages eleven to fourteen. The son had recently told his parents about the abuse, and now they wanted to hold the abuser accountable.[1]

The person they named was still active at church, and Mayberry knew him well. He took the man to lunch in a public place and confronted him. The man admitted that the accusation was true. Mayberry's next move was to tightly control who had access to this information—the man's identity, the fact that he admitted the abuse, the long-term nature of the abuse, and the age and gender of the victim.

The pastor's stated goal was to orchestrate a reconciliation between the abuser and his victim. He told the session (the church's governing board, composed of elders) that abuse had been committed in connection with the church, but he did not identify the abuser, saying that to do so would cause harm to the victim. He urged the elders to rely on his pastoral discretion and wisdom. The minutes from the session meeting in February of 1997 record that the unnamed "perpetrator, who appears suicidal, is in an intensive program of therapy and counseling, and he has met with his victim."[2]

THE ROLE OF THE CHURCH ELDERS

Mayberry acted as an autocratic head, one who could control outcomes. The elders, for their part, acquiesced to their pastor's unilateral handling of the situation. In so doing, they shirked their responsibilities to the body.

From its beginning, the governance model of the Presbyterian Church (USA) has called for elders and pastors to lead the church in partnership. The concept of elder—tending the flock "in your charge"—comes from 1 Peter 5. For Presbyterians, elders and pastors are both officers in the church. Their duties were laid out in 1788 in the denomination's Historic Principles, which states,

> That our blessed Savior, for the edification of the visible church, which is his body, hath appointed officers, not only to preach the gospel and administer the Sacraments but also to exercise discipline, for the preservation of both truth and duty; and that it is incumbent upon these officers, and upon the whole church, in whose name they act, *to censure or cast out the erroneous and scandalous*, observing, in all cases, the rules contained in the Word of God.[3] (emphasis added)

Instead of censuring the erroneous and scandalous, the elders acted like a weak corporate board deferring to an intimidating CEO. And because of their negligence, the situation worsened. During that same month, February 1997, PPC hired the abuser's wife onto its staff. But no one doing the hiring—other than the pastor—knew the abuser's identity.

At the same time, Mayberry *did* disclose the abuser's identity to select individuals, even though they weren't serving in leadership roles. So certain church insiders possessed confidential knowledge while the church leaders were kept in the dark. The church polity, which was designed to function as a safeguard for the health of the body, was not used as intended. The insiders should have urged the pastor to disclose information to the session. For their part, the session should have insisted that the pastor disclose information so they could lead the church in partnership. Indeed, because Mayberry kept them in the dark and they failed to act, the elders could be seen as being complicit in the abuse.

THE PASTOR RESPONDS TO THE ABUSE

The next month, Mayberry reached out to the regional church for advice and resources. He swore to secrecy the person assisting him before he divulged the nature of the problem. That individual referred him to Reverend James S. Evinger, a nationally recognized expert in sexual boundary violations in faith communities, who happened to live in the area.[4] Before talking to Evinger, Mayberry swore him to secrecy as well.

Evinger urged Mayberry to disclose information to the PPC session. Evinger also recommended a host of professional materials from the Interfaith Sexual Trauma Institute, Alban Institute, and what is now called FaithTrust Institute.[5] These resources draw on evidence-based research to provide best practices for situations involving sexual abuse. Mayberry rejected the advice, emphasizing what he saw as the uniqueness of the situation at PPC. He refused to involve law enforcement and asserted that none of the recommended procedures applied to this case because the abuser was not the typical abuser.

New York state law did not require the pastor's reporting of the abuse, and Mayberry repeatedly told Evinger that disclosure of any facts would not proceed until the victim was ready. This meant that the pastor simultaneously shielded the abuser and laid a weighty burden on the shoulders of a traumatized young man—a vulnerable member of the body. The pastor's action was self-protective: if his intended scenario of a grand reconciliation succeeded, he would be the hero; if it failed, he could say the young man was not ready. But this strategy kept the young man isolated. I know that many in the congregation, had they known, would have reached out to him and his family with care, understanding, and support. Most significantly—and likely revealing his true motives—Mayberry's strategy created a veil for his own actions and inactions. It would prove to carry grave consequences for others who were vulnerable.

Ignoring Evinger's recommendations and materials, Mayberry hired a secular consultant. He also circulated to the session an article supplied by the abuser's counselor titled "Community Notification and Setting the Record Straight on Recidivism."[6] The article downplayed the risk of re-offending and emphasized that sex offenders often face difficulties upon release from prison, such as "hate crimes. Public paranoia. Violence. Selective denial of human rights. Creation of a new criminal underclass." The article also referenced undocumented research that said first time offenders are unlikely to reoffend. By choosing to rely on the article, Mayberry placed other pre-adolescents at risk, both in the church and the church-sponsored Boy Scout troop. What's more, he cloaked his actions under the spiritualized value of ministering to the abuser, even though he was betraying the church's children and leading the elders to do the same.

The session followed Mayberry's wishes by both passive agreement and active votes. But, of course, people were talking. The information had leaked through unofficial channels. Pressure built to say *something*. So in May, the session called a congregational meeting to inform the church members that abuse had been committed by someone in their midst. The abuser's identity was not disclosed, nor were any particulars about the age and gender of the victim. Four years later the learning task force came to the following conclusion about that congregational meeting: "The explicit message to the congregation was that the leadership was prudent and vigilant, and the implicit message was that the congregation was safe. The opposite, however, was true. In relation to the perpetrator, there was a lack of vigilance by the leadership. The perception of safety was illusory."[7]

WHAT CONSTITUTES CONFESSION?

This statement was read aloud at the congregational meeting: "The [unnamed] offender has voluntarily *confessed* and voluntarily entered therapy, is permanently excluded from activities involving young people in this church, but by Session's prayerful decision, remains a member in our church's *care*" (emphasis mine). The elders signed off on this statement, noting that they, also, did not know the identity of the abuser.

Note that the statement uses the verb *confessed*, with all the religious and legal connotations of that word. What the abuser did, more accurately, was admit to certain facts. He did not admit culpability. To say, "yes, that happened," is different from acknowledging moral responsibility and being held accountable. A private conversation does not constitute confession in either a legal or religious sense. Presbyterians, like other Protestants, do not have a sacrament of confession that confers a veil of silence. True confession is followed by repentance and change of behavior, which begins building the bridge to forgiveness and restoration. It's key to note that in this case the pastor began construction on the forgiveness bridge prematurely. The abuser did nothing, although the bridge proved to be very convenient for him.

Making an untimely push toward so-called reconciliation is a way religious people commonly deal with wrong doing. Real reconciliation lies at the end of a long road and is rarely achieved. It involves the pursuit of accountability and justice, which takes time and intentionality. Like too many church leaders, Mayberry acted as if the whole messy business could be dispatched with a few choice words, as if *reconciliation* is a magic spell or a sprinkling of pixie dust. But Mayberry was worse than naive. He willfully ignored wise counsel, which caused grievous harm.

And what about the abuser? He was not well-served by the pastor's actions, as we will see. The statement read at the congregational meeting said that the church was showing *care* to the offender but without holding him (or her) accountable. This was a farce.

The purpose of the document and the congregational meeting was not to address the evil in their midst but to avoid the cognitive dissonance often felt in these situations: *How can such an awful thing happen in my church? Smooth it over, please.* Unfortunately, this is an unspoken but common goal within many congregations, even after serious misconduct.

EXTENDING THE BODY METAPHOR

Since the body of Christ is made up of more members than just eyes, hands, head, and feet, it can be helpful to extend Paul's metaphor. The body manages the critical functions of breathing, thanks to the lungs, and blood pumping to the organs, thanks to the heart. It also has skin to protect it, a skeletal system to support it, and an immune system to defend it. The immune system is incredibly complex, made up not only of lymph nodes, spleen, liver, and kidneys, but also bone marrow and white blood cells, the blood-brain barrier, and the entire gastrointestinal tract.

My husband and I have occasionally attended a "mini-medical school" for ordinary citizens at Georgetown School of Medicine. I will always be grateful for the opportunity to explore a cadaver in a lab that felt as sacred as a sanctuary, the smell of incense replaced by formaldehyde. At one lecture an immunologist said that the human body is so constantly attacked by disease that it's amazing it ever retains any health at all. And at the same time, the human body is so well-defended, with such complex and redundant protective systems, that it's amazing it ever experiences a day of sickness. According to the expert, both statements were equally true; it was just a matter of which lens you wanted to apply.

I have pondered that. As a member of the body of Christ, I ask myself, *Which way do I want to be amazed: by the constant onslaught of disease or by the body's robust defenses?* I know that

I'm tired of being shocked by depravity. I'm soul-sick that churches give sanctuary to abusers or pass them along to other bodies. I want to vomit when I hear of child victims who tried to stop their abuse but adults would not listen. These stories make me think the first lens is the right one, that health in the body of Christ is impossible.

But then I remind myself what I believe: that Jesus is the great healer, the source of love and miraculous power. I believe in the resurrection of the body, both his and ours. We who seek to be the body of Christ have access to love and healing power. We can become more aware of the disease around us and defend against it. As we build resistance we increase the body's health. If the second lens is true, we can choose health and hope.

SKIN, SKELETON, AND IMMUNE SYSTEM

What do the skin, skeleton, and immune system of the body of Christ look like? Skin is the body's largest organ, its first line of defense. Skin responds to external temperature. Maybe the members of the body who take on the role of skin are the ones who can be thick-skinned when necessary. They conduct interviews, contact references, and review background checks. They ask tough questions. They alert the body with shivers when something is wrong.

The body has a skeletal system to support it, including the rib cage, which wraps around so many precious organs. Protecting the vulnerable is key. Maybe the body's ribs are the nursery workers, Sunday school teachers, and youth group volunteers. They not only voice a commitment to protecting the vulnerable, they also put themselves on the line. They receive ongoing training and vow to maintain the safeguards that protect the vulnerable. They would rather crack than let anything damage what they protect.

The immune system is made up of many parts. The lymph nodes, which filter out bacteria and cancer particles, are linked together in a system. Maybe the lymph nodes are the multiple members who receive boundary training. They are poised to notice potential risks to the body and respond quickly through their linkages.

The spleen filters the blood. Is it happenstance that the apostle Paul wraps his Christology around the blood of Christ (see Romans 5:9)? It strikes me that this notion of keeping the blood clean is precisely what my Presbyterian forebears had in mind when they drafted their Historic Principles in 1788. Maybe the elders are the spleen, the blood filters—or the liver and kidneys, which also have a detoxifying function. The continuous cleaning these organs perform keep the body from being overwhelmed by toxins. When one of these organs begins to fail, a patient needs dialysis. Without dialysis, health declines precipitously. Maybe one of the body's crucial roles is accepting help and expertise from the outside when necessary.

Overall, some of these bodily functions should be filled by specific roles built into the church's structure, while others should be redundantly filled by as many individuals as possible. A church that creates and fills these strategic roles and also promotes heightened awareness of threats to the body will have begun to create an immune *system*.

In the case of PPC, it was the liver that failed. Assistance was offered by Evinger but was rejected with disastrous results. Refusing dialysis meant that toxins built up and spread through the system, poisoning another child.

AFTER THE CONGREGATIONAL MEETING

A representative from the regional church attended that congregational meeting in May 1997. This clergywoman was dis-
turbed by what she witnessed and wrote a substantial letter to
the session of PPC. Her words were both wise and prophetic. If
heeded, they might have prevented the tragedy to come.

> I am concerned that revealing so little may actually erode
> trust in a community over time, rather than restore and
> build trust. . . . There can be little "healing" if even the
> location of the "wound" is not known. I am concerned
> that this "solution" is not tenable if any other incidents
> of abuse occurred. You have built a zone of protection
> around the perpetrator. Can other victims come forward
> if they perceive that doing so may upset the carefully en-
> gineered "solution"? I worry that what you've done out of
> a desire to protect the perpetrator may postpone the for-
> giveness and healing you so desire. I also question the
> wisdom of entrusting a small group of those "who know"
> with the task of insuring that such behavior does not
> recur—not that those folks are untrustworthy, but that
> ultimately none of us can be responsible for the behavior
> of others, even if we could be everywhere at once.[8]

Nothing in the session's minutes indicates that the elders and
pastor ever discussed these perceptive words.

Mayberry did reach out to another colleague, John, the
pastor who contacted me by phone some eighteen months
later. (Apparently our conversation was not official, as no
notes appear in the case file.) For *two more years* Mayberry
functioned like a maestro in front of an orchestra, determining

who knew what, when. Even more significant, during that time he completely lost touch with the abuser, who no longer attended worship services and did not return the pastor's phone calls. Mayberry's supposed safeguards were a sham. Yet the session minutes continued to report that the church leaders exercised prudence and vigilance and that the congregation was safe. Such reports continued up until Mayberry left his position in May of 1999.

In February 1999, spurred by Mayberry's announcement that he intended to leave, the session created an ad hoc task force charged with managing the arrangement with the abuser. Evinger, in his role with the regional church, attended the first meeting of the task force. He pressed Mayberry to disclose the name of the abuser, which he did, very reluctantly. Evinger urged the task force to formally request that he be assigned to meet with the task force on an ongoing basis, but the pastor stalled that action. Until his departure in May, Mayberry led the task force meetings without using an agenda or creating minutes. Again, he sought to control outcomes by controlling the process.

Once Mayberry left, the task force assumed self-leadership and radically altered strategy. The importance of their courageous work cannot be overstated. Without these lay leaders, the identity of the abuser may never have been disclosed. They functioned as skin, bone, and immune system all at once, protecting, supporting, and defending the body. The task force's integrity and good work reinforces the wisdom of the partnership model of leadership intended by the denomination's governing documents. The consequences of Mayberry's Lone Ranger style of leadership were costly. Treating a specific incidence of abuse, or a certain known abuser, as somehow special and outside the norm is not only foolish but actually sinful. Evil acts flowed in the wake of Mayberry's "strategy."

ANOTHER BOMBSHELL

During the summer of 1999, the task force held two special meetings with the session. In July they disclosed the name of the offender to the elders, and in August they presented a motion to disclose the name to the congregation. The session voted to do so at a congregational meeting in mid-September.

As plans for that congregational meeting were underway, Mayberry's paid consultant revealed that another victim had come forward during the past year. Mayberry had known of this victim, as had one of the interim copastors and select church insiders. The existence of a second victim contradicted what Mayberry had told both the session and the congregation about the containment of the abuse.

Immediately after the congregational meeting, two more victims came forward. Like the first victim, each had been abused for multiple years in the 1980s.

As bad as that is, it gets worse. Not only did Mayberry's veil of secrecy keep other victims from coming forward sooner, but it created cover for the abuser to prey upon yet another child, "Victim 5."

While Mayberry was busy orchestrating the flow and blockage of information, the abuser had groomed and abused another boy, a member of PPC he had known since infancy. The abuser gained access to this child by first grooming the single mother, who felt the need for a strong, male role model for her son. Manipulated and misled, she entrusted her son to the abuser, who was a reputable leader at PPC and well-regarded for his relationships with youth. Over the course of the next two plus years, the abuser repeatedly raped this child.

In fact, court records show that the abuser began to commit acts against Victim 5 *within two weeks* of Mayberry circulating the article on recidivism in March of 1997. Clearly, the pedophile exploited the opportunity afforded by the pastor's strategy.[9] Cloaked by anonymity, he preyed on a member of the church that he, along with the rest of the congregation, had vowed to nurture in faith at his baptism—truly a heinous fact.

The second heinous fact is that the abuser had access to the child because Mayberry consciously chose to ignore all the best practices in the field. Perhaps the pastor fantasized that he could "save" his friend. In reality, his "care" for the abuser was nothing but leniency. His gullibility led him to shelter an abuser. His unwillingness to look at evil caused him to enlarge that evil.

The story continued when a sixth victim came forward. Who knows if more victims remain hidden?

To call Mayberry "misguided" and the session "ineffective" does not convey the enormity of their mistakes. Evil resides in the actions and inactions of people who fear the wrong thing: who fear exposing evil when they should fear complicity with evil, who fear damage to reputation when they should fear damage to the vulnerable, who fear the demands of pursuing justice when they should fear the consequences of not doing so.

SICKNESS IN THE BODY

The suffering of the body of Christ is real and needs to inform both our theology and practice. Certainly PPC suffered greatly when it allowed an abuser to flourish in their midst for years. At least six of their own children suffered repeated sexual abuse. When the abuse was exposed, the suffering spread like a virus as guilt affected every member of the body. The agony intensified at the revelation that at least some of the abuse could have been prevented. A healthy body rejects infection and protects its vulnerable members. Had this body been healthy, the session and pastor would have informed police and local authorities as soon as they were alerted of abuse. The pedophile would not have had access to Victim 5.

Some might ask, Wasn't the abuser also a member of the body? Wasn't the pastor trying to protect *him*? And that is true. In fact, the pastor was *highly invested* in protecting the abuser. He did so even though the abuser was not vulnerable, but instead powerful, and had harmed vulnerable ones.

Mayberry's actions elevated care for one member over care for another. He chose wrongly. He gave preferential treatment to the member who needed accountability. Instead of ejecting the disease, he protected the sore spot, the way a person limps to favor an aching knee. What the body needed was an intervention: surgery or crutches followed by a careful plan of rehabilitation.

When the body rejected treatment and sabotaged the immune response, the evil multiplied, like cancer cells. This is what evil does. It breeds crime. Call the multiplying process "disease" or call it "sin." The language matters less than the willingness to open our eyes and see the process at work.

Churches are systems in which members play key roles. Once alerted that infection is present, leaders must marshal an immune response, an intervention, a treatment.

Perhaps PPC's immune system was already weak. Certainly my encounter with the personnel committee a decade earlier showed a lackluster response to infection. Instead of confronting the harm, they ejected the one who alerted them to its existence.

Even though leaders turned over—Bolinger retired and Mayberry was hired—the head had not really changed. A similar leadership style persisted. The body expected an autocratic head and drew one to itself.

How does sickness snowball? Why does evil attract evil? What makes sinners of like mind cluster? Here's what I have observed. When a predator enters a system he (or she) sends out signals to see how the system will react. He takes liberties— small ones at first. His interactions are too familiar. He conveys an aura of being above the rules, often striking an attitude that's effective because it's disingenuous: *What, don't you trust me?* This is institutional grooming.

Unfortunately, an "above reproach" attitude plays especially well in churches, where people are too trusting and too quick to buy into the high and holy mission of the organization PPC was highly invested in having the "best" youth group around. That meant lots of laughs and not too many rules. Be spontaneous. Be lenient. Have fun! This attitude went so far as to become a form of idolatry.

THE HEALING COMMITTEE

After the task force disclosed the name of the abuser at a congregational meeting in September of 1999, the interim pastors suggested that the session disband the task force, which they did. But the ugly chapter was far from over. As previously mentioned, two victims immediately came forward. The very next month, Victim 5 reported recent abuse to law enforcement, who opened an investigation. Some of the former task force members who supported Victim 5 realized there was more to be done, so in November the session, upon Evinger's recommendation, created a healing committee and asked Evinger to serve as a consultant. That committee operated for fifteen months, cooperating fully with the investigation by state police. When they attempted to obtain information from Mayberry, he stonewalled them. Undeterred, the healing committee conducted listening meetings with members of the congregation. They held up the church's new core values of telling the truth and protecting vulnerable people.

In March of 2001, the committee's work culminated in a healing worship service open to the public. As circumstances would have it, this meeting took place two days after the abuser finally pled guilty. Several months later he was sentenced to jail time. As a registered sex offender, his identity was disclosed to all the world.

THE ABUSER REVEALED

The first time I saw his mug shot, my stomach roiled. I knew this face, slightly pudgy and framed by wispy hair, a face both familiar and alien. This face belonged to a person I had served alongside, a person who committed evil acts against the very children I had vowed to nurture in Christ. His name was Robert Gomperts.[10]

As I learned the pieces of this long, sad story, I alternated between rage and self-blame. For a restless season, I dreamed about the three tumultuous years I served at PPC. The culture of that church had always felt slippery and riddled with boundary violations, even beyond Bolinger's assault on me. That was why I had kept my antenna activated those three years, a habit that cost me in multiple ways—personally in sleepless nights and professionally in the hostility and scorn of those who saw me as uptight.

But in all those years I never suspected Gomperts. He was serving with the youth program when I arrived and continued for my three years. He was never much help in the planning phases, but the kids loved him. His wife directed the children's choir and organized the Christmas pageants, where my daughters wore tinsel halos. The Gomperts' own two children were teenagers then. My family even borrowed their camper for a summer week so that we could serve as managers at a church camp in the Finger Lakes. Bob had been eager to lend out the RV for a good cause. He was agreeable, jovial, carefree, and fun-loving.

I pored over the documents that came out of this case, especially the 2001 report from the learning task force, *From Pain to Hope*. A timeline in that report spanned the years I served as associate pastor, from 1990 to 1993, when I attempted to institute boundaries into the system. Of the victims that came forward, none reported experiencing abuse during that time. This became something like a life-raft in my sea of self-blame. Maybe my efforts had made a difference?

Yet, even though my antenna was on alert, I had not suspected Gomperts. The truth is that I watched the men with the girls. It didn't occur to me that a man might prey on boys. In hindsight, that is remarkably naive. Meanwhile I'd been quick to pounce on a volunteer who was overly familiar with girls. I lamented to my husband that I'd been suspicious of the wrong man, someone innocent. Doug reminded me that I should be cautious with the word *innocent*. "It's one thing to be guilty and another to be caught." I realized he was right. Only God knows everything that went on at PPC.

BODIES PROTECT WHAT THEY IDOLIZE

Idolatry lays the groundwork for sexual abuse. Idolatry crops up in every system, including nonreligious ones. Every system reveres something. Maybe it's money, power, fame, or influence. There's some sort of golden ring that people want to grasp. If an abuser has a strong hold on that golden ring, the whole system can protectively wrap itself around him. The system is not protecting the abuser per se—it's protecting everyone's share of that ring. Even the victim may believe in the power of the golden ring and be caught by its allure. At PPC, the golden ring was a thriving youth group that students wanted to join. Gomperts exploited that desire to feed his own evil purposes. Even when the system—the head of the body—knew he was a predator, it did not act decisively to stop him.

The events at PPC are heartbreaking and shocking but no longer surprising. Faith communities have been rocked by stories of pedophilic abuse and cover-up within the Roman Catholic Church and the Southern Baptist Convention. These stories pierce the soul. But any tight-knit faith community can become a breeding ground for abuse and secrecy, especially if it revolves around a charismatic leader, is reluctant to address issues of sexuality forthrightly, and is self-policed by an elite group.

In order to fight abuse, the body of Christ needs to have a strong immune *system*. One systemic problem is the lack of statistics about abuse. This is the first thing churches must remedy. Compiling statistics will reveal the scope of the problem, knowledge that will strengthen the body's immune response.

We can no longer think of abuse as being solely the work of sick individuals. That's too easy. We must examine the system that allowed a predator to thrive and hide. If we simply remove that individual without changing the system, a new predator may soon appear.

THE NEW POLICY IS TESTED

A few years after PPC redesigned its policy for handling allegations of sexual abuse, the policy met its first test. A church member was arrested for abusing his family members. The new pastor was able to refer to the policy and the church's core values, which served as a bulwark. She and church leaders handled the situation properly by supporting the abused family members in court.

Not long afterward, a youth member got in trouble for forcibly touching women in a community setting. He ended up in family court. Believing that the offense was minor, that the youth was sorry, and that the whole thing should be hushed, a number of church leaders went to court with the youth to support him. Even after their experience with Comperts, some leaders resisted having secrets exposed. However, the church leaders used the spirit of their new policy to disclose basic facts, including the youth's identity, to the congregation.

The takeaway here is that strengthening the immune system is a process and takes time. As Christians we live in hope, by the light of Jesus that dispels all darkness. The document from the learning task force, *From Pain to Hope,* clearly states its purpose: "This report is an act of discernment that is best understood as an act of discipleship as followers of Jesus Christ who calls us to learn from our travails, to live as witnesses to the truth, to serve as instruments of justice, and to minister as agents of healing."[11]

THE TEXT ASKS US

1. How will our body of Christ function as an organic, non-hierarchical system?

2. Which members are *weaker,* and how will we protect them?

MY HOPE

My hope is that the body of Christ will strengthen its immune system and proactively excise the cancers that invade it.

CHAPTER FOUR

ACCOUNTABILITY AND JUSTICE

There can be no love without justice.

BELL HOOKS, *ALL ABOUT LOVE: NEW VISIONS*

There was a widow who kept coming to him and saying, "Grant me justice against my opponent."

LUKE 18:3

MY PULSE JUMPED. The image on the large screen showed a person sitting on a precipice above a canyon. Below him, red and orange cliffs wore a dusting of snow, while just behind him, like a tethering post, stood a large fir tree, its green branches weighted with white. The person's precarious perch spoke to me, along with the solidity of the solo tree. We'd been asked to choose an image which represented our experience in ministry. To me the canyon and the fir tree combined riskiness and rootedness.

It was October 2009. I was attending a CREDO conference for "mid-career pastors," spending a week away from ministry to reflect on my vocation. After nearly twenty years in ministry, I was supposed to ask myself, Where was I, and how had God been with me as I got here? What about the past remained unfinished? Where did the Spirit call me next?

Given the gift of time and space to reflect, I became aware that I had two hidden pockets of unfinished business. Both contained sexual assault.

In one pocket was my history of being raped at gunpoint in college, which still held tremendous power over my inner life. When I dared to share this part of my past, people seemed uneasy. The sense was, why disclose such a tender thing? But I was beginning to question why silence was necessary. What if the trauma had been a car accident or cancer diagnosis? That information would be received differently. Was my own anxiety around this story the residue of shame? Would I never be free of that burden? I began to wonder if the Spirit was calling me to do something with this trauma—something more than simply survive it.

The other pocket held the physical assault by my boss, Zane Bolinger, during my first years in ministry at Penfield Presbyterian Church (PPC) some sixteen years previous. The two assaults—rape in my home in 1978 and a forcible kiss in my church office in 1991—felt connected.

As part of the deep, interior work of the conference, I made a timeline of the aftermath of the rape at gunpoint. Early on, justice had played a key role in my healing, even though it felt cumbersome at the time. The legal process was repeatedly delayed. Waiting to testify at the trial had been its own time of trial.

But testifying had shifted me from victim to plaintiff, from powerless to powerful. I have body memories of taking the witness stand, my corduroy skirt swishing around my knees. I can still see the jurors dab their eyes; I can still look up at the black-robed judge in his high perch. The rapist was silent and guarded by bailiffs. When he broke into our home, he had wielded the power: a gun. But when my sister victims and I testified, we wielded the power with a different sort of weapon: our words. For us, the justice system really *did* procure justice.

Next on my timeline came beginnings: marriage, seminary, and motherhood. These were objective indicators of healing, of finding a life track. The fact that each of these threads continued decades later—my marriage, my ministry, my mothering—spoke to their tenacity.

Then came my first experience in ministry at PPC, a setback whose cost is hard to quantify. In an aha moment, I understood why my shame intensified then. Bolinger's abuse had included his fascination with my rape history. And when I brought the abuse to the attention of the PPC personnel committee, I was dismissed because my history as a rape survivor made me less credible. Meanwhile, my boss was given impunity.

Remembering the whole scenario could still anger me in a blink. Bolinger had vowed to encourage and guide me as a colleague in ministry. He was privileged to lay his hands on my head to ordain me. Then he clamped those same two hands on either side of my head to assault me. I couldn't square the images side-by-side. They created an abomination.

I had no doubt that Bolinger's abuse sabotaged my entrance into ministry, something I had worked toward for years. Meeting with PPC's hapless personnel committee only added insults. In order to protect myself, my marriage, and our children, I chose a lesser path professionally. Women often make these trade-offs. But my choices revolved around victimization in a way that felt particularly unjust.

As I prayed and meditated at the conference, I began to wonder if my discomfort with these memories was entirely negative. Maybe the restlessness came from God. Maybe the Spirit was spurring me to action. After all, the church—which I vowed to serve and spent decades serving—had failed to hear my cries. Wasn't it reasonable to demand a hearing? Every Sunday I preached about a God who loves justice, a Jesus who healed women as readily as he did men, and a Spirit whose presence is new every day. Maybe that same Spirit, who descended on me at ordination, was pushing me to pursue accountability and justice.

THE PARABLE OF THE PERSISTENT WIDOW AND THE UNJUST JUDGE

Jesus tells a story about a woman pursuing justice. After the introduction, the story takes only three sentences:

> Then Jesus told them a parable about their need to pray always and not to lose heart. He said, "In a certain city there was a judge who neither feared God nor had respect for people. In that city there was a widow who kept coming to him and saying, 'Grant me justice against my opponent.' For a while he refused; but later he said to himself, 'Though I have no fear of God and no respect for anyone, yet because this widow keeps bothering me, I will grant her justice, so that she may not wear me out by continually coming.'" (Luke 18:1-5)

In the lead-in to this parable Jesus sets out the meaning: "[the] need to pray always and not to lose heart." There's no doubt that persistence in prayer is an important topic in Luke's Gospel. He has already recorded the Ask, Seek, Knock passage, which has a similar theme (Luke 11:5-13). What's more, on three occasions Luke specifically mentions that Jesus withdrew to pray.[1] Is this parable a reinforcement of the teaching about prayer, or might Jesus be communicating something more?

Another reason to wonder is that no other parable is explained before it begins. Parables work in the opposite direction: as soon as the reader grasps the point, something upends that interpretation. Parables are meant to puzzle us, to disarm us, to challenge our thinking. Each phrase is precious, a potential window into a surprising way of thinking, a way more like Jesus. We receive a parable as a gift to ponder. A parable cannot be summarized in an introductory line, or it wouldn't need to be told.

CASTING QUANDARIES

This parable features just two characters, but their identity presents a puzzle. If the point is to "pray always" as the text says, then we, the hearers, are cast as the persistent widow demanding justice. But doesn't that cast *God* as the unjust judge? It seems an odd role for Jesus to assign to the Almighty, the One who will judge the heavens and the earth.

And why does Jesus choose a widow as his protagonist? This character demands "justice against my opponent" (Luke 18:3). In Jesus' day, women had few legal rights, and those few were accessed through the males in her family—a father, husband, brother, or son. To choose a widow as the one demanding justice is a perplexing, even outrageous choice. Without male relatives, this widow has no legal standing.

Since male relatives are also a widow's only hedge against poverty, widows play the role of vulnerable ones in Scripture. They're often lumped together with orphans and aliens—people who need special protection. The Hebrew word for widow is *al-manah,* which derives from the verb *alma,* to be bound like an animal. Over time the meaning shifted from being bound to being made dumb, or mute. So the word *widow* includes the notion of being silenced, by others or by circumstance.

Through his casting choices, Jesus reverses the typical societal roles. Not only is the mighty judge—the dispenser of justice—unjust, but the person issuing demands is vulnerable. Let the surprise of that reversal sink in. A person who typically needs protection *from* her opponent is demanding justice *against* her opponent. Actually, if you're acquainted with Jesus and his topsy-turvy ways, it's not that surprising—outrageous maybe but not surprising.

Jesus was born from these kinds of reversals. His teenage mother sang a song of overturning when she found out she was pregnant—even though she was in a very difficult circumstance. It's no surprise that it's Luke who records her song:

> He [the Mighty One] has brought down the powerful
> > from their thrones,
> > and lifted up the lowly;
> he has filled the hungry with good things,
> > and sent the rich away empty. (Luke 1:52-53)

Mary's song was the overture to Jesus' life, the musical theme announced before he made his appearance. His life played out that theme as he spent his ministry unsettling the social order, overturning the status quo, tipping the tables, and toppling the powerful.

Throughout the Gospels we see Jesus' special interest in the vulnerable ones, the poor, the orphaned, the widowed, and the aliens. Since a concern for the vulnerable runs through the Hebrew scriptures—from the letter of the Law to the words of the prophets—what's unique about Jesus is not a theoretical concern but the freedom and energy his words and actions convey when dealing with those who are poor, sick, or cast aside.

In Luke, Jesus interacts with widows from his first days. Anna, an aged widow who lives in the temple, prophesies that the infant Jesus will bring about the redemption of Jerusalem (Luke 2:36-38).

While preaching in Nazareth, his hometown, Jesus mentions the widow of Zarephath, who fed Elijah in the desert, a story that would have been well-known to his audience (see 1 Kings 17). Jesus lauds the widow as being more deserving than the people he was addressing. There's no misunderstanding Jesus' implication: a "worthless" widow is worthier than them. To say this angers the crowd is an understatement. The mob tries to throw Jesus off a precipice, a form of public execution (Luke 4:25-30).

Later in Luke's Gospel, Jesus praises the widow who donates two pennies, the only coins she owns. That praise is a condemnation of the opposite behavior, the conspicuous offerings of wealthy and powerful religious leaders (Luke 21:1-4).

In Luke 7, Jesus is approaching a town and sees a funeral procession leaving the town gates, headed for the cemetery. The young man who died was a widow's only son. Jesus has compassion, and as he passes the funeral bier, he stops the procession in its tracks. He speaks over the corpse: "Young man, I say to you, rise!" Then the text says, in typically understated fashion, "The dead man sat up and began to speak, and Jesus gave him to his mother" (Luke 7:11-17).

Luke makes it clear that Jesus doesn't look at widows the same way other people do. He responds to them with compassion but not with pity. He increases their agency and power. In that context, it makes sense that Jesus would cast a vulnerable woman, a widow, in the title role of his drama about the pursuit of justice.

BRINGING THE DISCIPLINARY CASE: MY STORY

In March of 2010, I used the Presbyterian disciplinary process to bring an allegation against Zane Bolinger, my former boss. Reverend James S. Evinger helped me navigate the ecclesiastical procedures.[2] Seventeen years had elapsed since Bolinger assaulted me, and I'm sure he was surprised to receive those papers. Isn't this type of retroactive legal action the reason people push back against the #MeToo movement? But note the date: I took this action seven years before #MeToo became a hashtag. According to the Presbyterian Rules of Discipline, the charge of "sexual abuse of another person" has no statute of limitations. (At the time, the category of sexual harassment did not exist.)

An investigating committee (IC) was formed. When the IC interviewed the former members of the PPC personnel committee, individuals recalled my telling them about the forcible kiss and Bolinger's admission of the same. In 2010 that behavior fell squarely under the rubric of "sexual abuse," so the case was open and shut—or so I thought.

In late August, the IC called to interview me. All five committee members were on the phone. I took copious notes, basically a transcription of what was said. The first question someone asked was, "How does forgiveness factor in?" One member spoke at length, indicating that a sincere Christian would not have initiated this disciplinary case. I replied, "Forgiveness and justice are two different things. If there's something for me to forgive, that means a wrong has been committed. That needs to be acknowledged."

The IC had no choice but to continue their investigation. A month later, they called to report that they had interviewed Bolinger. He admitted to the forcible kiss, though he characterized it as a "loving peck." He either had no cognizance that he abused me or was unwilling to admit it. By this time, the members of the IC agreed with my viewpoint that the forcible kiss was an act of sexual abuse. Further, they acknowledged that the abuse was part of a larger pattern of domination and control. But at the same time, they asked me to drop the case, saying it wouldn't "go anywhere" because: (1) too much time had passed, (2) there were no witnesses, (3) there was no documentation, and (4) the disciplinary action of censure would be meaningless because Bolinger was retired.

One member asked if an apology would suffice. What kind of apology did I require? On paper? In person? What would help me "heal and move on"?

I said that if Bolinger wrote down a generic "I'm sorry" with no real understanding or contrition, that would not be meaningful, especially if it were treated as a purely private matter. I wanted him to admit he abused his power. I also wanted a public component of setting the record straight, in case there were other victims.

After the phone call, I followed up with an email.[3] Here's how I responded to the four reasons they gave for pushing to drop the case:

1. Time. It's true that much time has passed, which only underscores the fact that this was a grievance that time did not heal. The accused and the accuser are still alive and in good health, so does the elapsed time matter? My earlier attempts at justice were thwarted by the Personnel Committee of the church.

2. Documentation. The lack of documentation is unsurprising, given the church's proclivity to cover up facts. We know that documentation did at one time exist and was removed from church files. Does this make the grievance less grievous?

3. Witnesses. It's true that no one else was in my office when Bolinger surprised me from behind, spun my chair around, and forcibly kissed me on the lips with a hand on either side of my head. However, there were many witnesses to Bolinger's inappropriate attentions to me because they extended for months and years. There are also witnesses to the fact that I called a meeting of the appropriate committee and told many elders about what had transpired. You have talked to some of these witnesses.

4. Censure. This merits more consideration. What is the purpose of censure? It is not primarily to protect future victims. The definition of Church Discipline in D-1.0101 reads, in part: "Thus the purpose of discipline is to honor God by making clear the significance of membership in the body of Christ; to preserve the purity of the church by nourishing the individual within the life of the believing community; to achieve justice and compassion for all participants involved; to correct or restrain wrong-doing in order to bring members to repentance and restoration; to uphold the dignity of those who have been harmed by disciplinary offenses." I believe that pursuing censure at this date will pursue these goals, especially that of achieving justice and compassion for me, the victim, and bringing the offender to repentance and restoration. The lowest form of censure is rebuke, which is not tied to a minister's continued service in the church and so applies to this situation.[4] In addition, D-12.0103(d) specifically states that "in a case in which the offense is sexual abuse of another person, the rehabilitation program may include the advice that the person found guilty complete a voluntary act or acts of repentance."

AN ATTORNEY ENTERS

Although he had admitted guilt, Bolinger hired an attorney to fight the charges. His attorney couldn't do much. Still, he generated paperwork and phone calls. The IC again asked me to drop the case, saying that I was taking up the denomination's valuable resources. That stung. I prayed about whether I should do as requested but felt led to say no. I told the IC that I wasn't the one who hired a lawyer and turned this into a protracted legal battle.

After some nine months, Bolinger finally agreed to plead guilty if we adopted an "Alternate Form of Resolution." This would sidestep some of the Rules of Discipline but yield similar results. For expediency, I agreed to it.

Bolinger's lawyer then asked me to sign a release from civil liability, saying that, in turn, Bolinger would file a release from defamation charges. I actually laughed when I read that. I responded that civil liability was moot because the statute of limitations in New York state had expired. As for Bolinger suing me for defamation, I wrote, "Not only does the truth set one free, it is an adequate legal defense." I also made the point that sandwiching a guilty plea between the pages of a release of liability lacked sincerity. What game was he playing? Either he had forcibly kissed me or not. Did he acknowledge his abusive act?

At this point, an attorney for the IC called and advised me to sign the release form. She said I would never receive anything more from Bolinger. I shook my head at the implication. What "more" did I want besides an apology? There was never any money on the line. The Rules of Discipline are clear that an ecclesiastical court cannot settle financial claims or award damages. It can only impose censure.

"All I want is for him to acknowledge his fault and sincerely apologize," I told the attorney.

The attorney replied that I was holding onto false hope. I would never receive an apology: "In my experience, perpetrators are notoriously immune to insight."

I couldn't immediately wrap my head around that phrase. Was "immune to insight" the same thing as hopeless? People who love Jesus don't *do* hopeless.

OPPONENTS AND BLACK EYES

Jesus doesn't fill in the details of his parable. We aren't told the nature of the widow's legal trouble, or even if she's in the right. Jesus does, however, address the widow's decorum. Does she pursue her cause like a "good girl"? Does she choose her words carefully and deliver them in a modulated tone during office hours? Not at all. The widow is annoying. She shows up at all hours of the day and night and bangs on her opponent's door: "In that city there was a widow who kept coming to him and saying, 'Grant me justice against my opponent'" (Luke 18:3).

Her *opponent*. When Jesus uses that word, it suggests that women can *have* opponents. Fancy that. Jesus doesn't suggest that the widow lower her expectations or lower her voice. Jesus doesn't suggest she come back in the morning after she's pulled herself together and can talk nicely. Apparently, her actions are nice enough for Jesus. Pounding on the door of the unjust judge is fine. Contrast that with 1 Corinthians 6:1-8, in which the apostle Paul exhorts Christians to avoid legal action, advice often used to keep abused women in line.

The judge, for his part, is self-important. Jesus says that the judge "neither feared God nor had respect for people" (Luke 18:2) and then has the judge restate the same: "'Though I have no fear of God and no respect for anyone'" (Luke 18:4). In this three-sentence story, one-and-a-half sentences make it clear that the judge is deplorably "unjust" (Luke 18:6). Such a character isn't about to be swayed by the widow's goodness, or purity, or the righteousness of her cause. Instead, he is swayed because she bothers him. She pesters him. She wears him down.

And here's one more key point. The parable's ending has a variant reading. The NRSV reads that the judge said, "Yet because this widow keeps bothering me, I will grant her justice, *so that she may not wear me out by continually coming*'" (Luke 18:5, emphasis added). A footnote links to an alternative wording for that last phrase, culled from other ancient manuscripts: "Or *so that she may not finally come and slap me in the face*." The

Greek used here is unusual in Scripture because it's essentially boxing terminology. Scholars suggest that the best translation of the sense of the phrase might be, *the woman is giving me a black eye.*

A black eye signifies a particular kind of problem—an image problem. A black eye is conspicuous. It invites questions. It suggests a brawl, a bar fight, a dispute settled in the alley. Maybe the judge relents because the widow has information that could embarrass him publicly. Maybe, as a public figure, he's simply defending his reputation. Is it reading into the text to wonder whether the judge ever laid hands on the widow? Whatever the case, the widow knew how to disrupt the judge's power and was willing to do so in a public way by banging on his door.

THE WHEELS OF JUSTICE

After two more months, Bolinger dropped the issue of the release documents. He signed the Alternate Form of Resolution. Those documents were forwarded to the permanent judicial commission (PJC), which functions as judge and jury in the Presbyterian system. This body is made up of rotating members who are church officers, both elders and pastors.

In May of 2011, the PJC rendered its decision. In part, the decision states,

> In the context of these relationships, the actions of Rev. Zane Bolinger, by breaking down set boundaries of professional fiduciary and ministerial relationships, were not only sexual abuse, but abuse of power. As an outcome of those actions, Rev. Ruth Everhart experienced harm, injury and/or damage in one or more of the following domains: physical, emotional, psychological, spiritual,

familial, financial, and occupational. The manifestation of such occurred not only during commission of the misconduct itself, but over time following commission.[5]

The PJC had the power to impose church censure. They chose not to revoke Bolinger's ministerial standing, telling me they didn't want to imperil his pension. If they thought this was true, they were mistaken or misled. A pastor who is stripped of his credentials cannot be stripped of the pension he has legally earned. Perhaps this red herring was the PJC's way of sidestepping the possibility of imposing a greater penalty.

Whatever their reason, the PJC chose the lowest form of censure: a rebuke to be read aloud during a closed meeting of the regional church. I was not invited to attend that meeting. Bolinger chose to skip it. Therefore, neither party heard the following public rebuke:

> Whereas you, Rev. Zane Bolinger, a minister of Word and Sacrament and member of Geneva Presbytery, have been found guilty of the offense of sexual abuse and by such offense you have acted contrary to the Scriptures and the Constitution of the Presbyterian Church U.S.A., now therefore the Geneva Presbytery, in the name and authority of the Presbyterian Church U.S.A., expresses its condemnation of this offense, and rebukes you. You are enjoined to be more watchful and avoid such offense in the future. We urge you to use diligently the means of grace to the end that you may be more obedient to our Lord Jesus Christ.

On the one hand, the PJC's finding was sobering. It ruled that Bolinger committed a serious offense. On the other hand, the discipline imposed was minimal. To my mind, the *public rebuke* was neither *public*, since it took place in a closed-door meeting in the absence of both the victim and victimizer, nor a *rebuke*, since it didn't describe the offense.

After a total of fourteen months of paperwork and negotiation, the experience ended with a non-public non-rebuke. A whimper. A dead-end. A dud. Technically, I had prevailed. But I was not even officially notified of the PJC's decision. I received no correspondence of any kind from Bolinger or PPC. As my husband sagely observed, everything to do with that church had been a disappointment, and this was no different. Even the vindication was, in his words, a "nothing burger."

CHANNELING THE WIDOW

The parable of the persistent, pestering widow comforted me as I went through the legal process. This parable offers encouragement to all who pursue justice, even those using methods that are socially unacceptable. The gospel truth is that the Mighty One sides with the vulnerable who disrupt power. Bringing embarrassment is a reasonable thing to do, even if the guilty party is powerful.

It's tempting to leave the pursuit of justice to others—let someone else persist and speak truth to power. It feels uncomfortable to be vocal, especially if we grew up with the message that women should be quiet and submissive. This parable sends a different, empowering message. Jesus lifts every vulnerable person from the margins and encourages her to seek her day in court.

By initiating disciplinary action, I attempted to hand the problem back to its rightful owner. I can't say I was successful, but I was persistent. And I can live with that.

THE CHURCH RESPONDS

The PJC rendered its decision in May 2011. In October I received a letter from the PPC session (the church's governing board) saying that the session "regrets that you felt that your narrative was not heard and responded to appropriately" and "empathizes with you." The letter closed with the assurance that the session would "pray for healing for you, Rev. Zane Bolinger, and the congregation."[6]

Curiously enough, the letter was dated August 22, 2011. I am unclear as to why delivery was delayed for six weeks. Still, it seemed fitting that I should have to wait a long time for a limp response. The session did not acknowledge wrongdoing, did not apologize, and did not invoke the word justice. It did not regret Bolinger's actions, even though he admitted guilt. It did not regret the church leaders' actions—and inactions—all those years ago.

Instead of looking at the power dynamics that created the situation, or the system's failure to respond when presented with the truth, the problem was framed as being about my *feelings*: the session "regrets that you *felt* that your narrative was not heard and responded to appropriately." Feelings of injustice are apparently easier to fix than actual injustices, especially if it's incumbent on the *victim* to do the fixing. The letter used the verb "empathize" although it did not do the work of empathy—or, what would be more appropriate—compassion and solidarity. To close by saying they would "pray for healing" simply underscores that the church did not know the difference between prayer and prayerful action. It had no stomach for doing hard work.

A person might wonder if the response was so minimal because the abuse was *just* a forcible kiss and not something more egregious. I could understand that reaction if someone focused only on that single moment. They might say: buck up, sister, life is hard! But the session had my whole story in writing.

It's more likely that the session minimized the abuse because it didn't want to face the issue of restitution. While the Rules of Discipline don't provide for monetary damages, an offer of restitution is certainly a reasonable follow-up to an admission of guilt. Nothing would have prohibited either the session or Bolinger from making such an offer. Churches undervalue the role of financial settlements, as if Christians are above such worldly concerns. Yet any divorce lawyer can tell you that a financial settlement is not just about money. Their clients are seeking justice, and possibly a reckoning, as a path to healing.

The session's lack of courage and integrity irritated me, so I decided to raise the issue overtly. I replied to the session asking if we could arrange a face-to-face meeting. I quantified the losses I suffered in terms of dollars and cents. I wrote a separate letter to Bolinger, with similar content. Bolinger never replied, but the session did, and speedily! Their reply was muscular. They "decline" a meeting, and "there will be no financial restitution." The wallop came in the closing. "Please know that this will be our final correspondence with you. However, we continue to pray that all affected by this situation may experience the wholeness and healing found in God."[7]

For those unfamiliar with churchy language, to wish someone "wholeness and healing" can also be translated as "kiss off!"

Darkly inspired, I wrote the following snarky article that never went anywhere beyond the confines of my computer:

7 Easy Steps for Churches Confronting Difficult Truths

1. *Avoid hearing the truth.* There are many effective types of earplugs, or you can simply clamp your hands over your ears. (I can't *hear* you!)

2. *Pretend you don't understand what's wrong.* (Everything is fine. Because Jesus!)

3. *Listen to the victim because they expect it.* (When they stop talking, forget everything!)

4. *Protect persons in power.* (Power begets power, and power is fun!)

5. *Remember there are two sides to every story.* (Choose the side that makes you the most comfortable!)

6. *If harm has been done, try using "Jesus" and "forgiveness" in the same sentence.* (Now the pain is all gone!)

7. *Resume business as usual.* (Back to #1, insert earplugs!)

SOMEBODY'S KNOCKING

Let's consider the widow's parable again, but this time turn the puzzle-package upside down. What if the persistent widow is not us, the readers, knocking on Jesus' door, but Jesus knocking on our churches' door? Of the two possibilities—Jesus or the church—we know who's more likely to be the unjust judge.

This alternate interpretation is echoed by a well-loved verse: "Listen, I am standing at the door, knocking" (Revelation 3:20).

In Revelation, John shares a vision of the Spirit reproving each of the seven churches in Asia. The church at Laodicea has been *lukewarm*. I wonder if it's been lukewarm in pursuing justice.

> I know your works; you are neither cold nor hot. I wish that you were either cold or hot. So, because you are lukewarm, and neither cold nor hot, I am about to spit you out of my mouth. (Revelation 3:15-16)

To the Spirit, this detestable lukewarm state is connected to material wealth—or at least a preoccupation with material wealth—that functions as blinders to the church's actual wretchedness. Fortunately, there is a remedy.

> For you say, "I am rich, I have prospered, and I need nothing." You do not realize that you are wretched, pitiable, poor, blind, and naked. Therefore I counsel you to buy from me *gold refined by fire* so that you may be *rich*; and *white robes* to clothe you and to keep the shame of your nakedness from being seen; and *salve* to anoint your eyes so that you may see. I *reprove and discipline* those whom I love. Be earnest, therefore, and repent. (Revelation 3:17-19, emphasis added)

The remedy to being lukewarm is to add some heat: *reproof and discipline*. The church can participate in this work by repenting. This involves a complete strip-down and overhaul of the value system. What the church needs is *gold refined by fire*. This might suggest, among other things, the precious wisdom of those who've been refined by the fire of abuse.

It may cost the church something to listen to victims and survivors, but it will make them *rich,* able to buy the necessary *white robes* and *salve.* Can churches admit that they are *blind and naked*? Too often churches act as if they're the dispensary instead of the blind patient, as if they own the garment district when they are naked, exposed to all the world.

Yes, there will be costs involved, both monetary and societal. (Note that costs are mounting even without repentance. The church has lost its status as trustworthy.) And keep reading— the potential gain is tremendous, a place at the table.

> Listen! I am standing at the door, knocking; if you hear my voice and open the door, I will come in to you and eat with you, and you with me. To the one who conquers I will give a place with me on my throne, just as I myself con- quered and sat down with my Father on his throne. Let anyone who has an ear listen to what the Spirit is saying to the churches. (Revelation 3:20-22)

Could Jesus be knocking to invite the church to repentance as part of justice? He'll knock *on* the door, but he won't knock *down* the door. Churches will have to open up. They will have to exercise collective agency—hear the knock, open the door, and invite Jesus to the table. Then they will feast with the resurrected Lord.

This passage is a picture of what the church *does have*—that the secular #MeToo culture does *not*—this vision of the throne (Revelation 3:21). The church can glimpse Jesus, seated on the throne of glory, and hear the invitation to join him. This in- volves a reorientation toward power and its trappings of wealth. Jesus has no reverence for riches, at least not the kind that fold into a wallet. Instead Jesus raises a fist to knock on the church's door. To open that door will mean seeing the world through his eyes—as a place where the vulnerable have value, the powerless have power, and the feast begins.

WHAT I LEARNED FROM MY FORAY THROUGH CHURCH COURTS

I learned that doing justice is a complex concept. Justice mandates that we give persons what is rightfully theirs. This applies in a legal sense to punishment or vindication. But it might also mean to restore social standing, provide financial support, or convey respect and dignity. The work of justice is to discern what's due and ensure that the person receives it.

I learned to be suspicious when Christians talk about healing without mentioning justice. Justice is one of the pathways to healing. Healing is too often treated as an ephemeral feeling-state rather than a by-product of pursuing justice. This misconception lays all the responsibility for healing on the victim.

I learned to value apology as a building block of confession and repentance. I was profoundly disappointed that I received no apology from either the church leaders or Bolinger. What does it mean when a person is cornered into admitting guilt and still refuses to say they're sorry? And I wasn't the only one who deserved an apology. Not only did Bolinger manhandle me, he was the leader of a dysfunctional system that bred exponentially greater abuse. Bolinger's actions caused dire consequences to people other than himself, yet he made no amends.

I learned that all churches struggle with holding clergy accountable, no matter their form of government. The Roman

Catholic scandals show that a hierarchical structure can hide offenses and offenders. The Southern Baptist scandals show that loose affiliations can allow offenders to move between churches unchecked. But my experience shows that a connectional system—blending hierarchy and lay power through a representative democracy—is also flawed. Since the problem of abuse persists across various structures, structural change alone isn't the solution. While each structure can, and must, adapt to respond to this #MeToo reckoning, the norms of church culture must also change. In every structure the attitude of individuals who occupy leadership positions is key.

I learned that the church confuses justice and fiscal responsibility. Pursuing justice can be expensive, which is a stumbling block for churches. My denomination, for one, is shackled to a lawyerly mindset. But concern for fiscal liability is an inadequate justice framework. Christian communities must learn how to embody the kingdom realities of confession, repentance, forgiveness, and reconciliation.

I learned that when church courts are modeled on civil courts, they treat offenses as violations of rules rather than betrayals of relationships. Churches are faith communities, so their values and norms should be different from those of secular society. Churches comprise the body of Christ, a group of people gathered in covenant relationship. Relationships should be non-exploitative and based in love for the truth. Since current secular justice systems are adapting truth-telling techniques such as "victim impact statements," a religious body that cherishes the power of personal testimony can certainly learn to incorporate similar techniques.

I learned that power dynamics are slow to shift. When I was assaulted in my church office, I was powerless. When I asked the personnel committee for help, I was treated with pity but not compassion. Apparently it was my problem, connected to my prior victimization: *Poor Ruth!* When I brought the accusation, I exercised power. I prevailed in court. Yet the church correspondence continued to treat the problem as belonging to me, to my inability to heal. I was still *Poor Ruth*, the pathetic clergywoman who refused to move on from the past. I find it remarkable that as soon as I claimed my power, the church abrogated theirs. The session could have responded in a way that brought more justice into the situation, but they lacked the courage to do so.

I learned that many people equate healing with silence. I sometimes receive messages from people who hope I will finally find healing. While I don't believe they intend to convey condescension, what they unintentionally echo is the premise at the heart of my memoir: that when a woman is raped, she is viewed as permanently damaged. To some people, the rape stain has apparently lingered on me some forty years—since I'm still writing about it. The implication is that when I'm healed I will stop writing about sexual assault. In other words, their goal is my silence. I can say that I'm fairly well healed (though not well-heeled—ha!). Still, I will keep writing about this subject because God called me to it. My goal is nothing less than culture change, which cannot be achieved with silence.

THE TEXT ASKS US

1. Who is your opponent? Are you sure that's the right one?
2. How persistent are you in accosting your opponent?

MY HOPE

My hope is that the church can harness the persistence and energy of a widow who feels wronged in order to pursue justice for the vulnerable who have been sexually abused.

CHAPTER FIVE

PURITY CULTURE AND RAPE CULTURE

Women do not get raped because they weren't careful enough. Women get raped because someone raped them.

JESSICA VALENTI, *THE PURITY MYTH*

But the thing that David had done displeased the LORD.

2 SAMUEL 11:27

WHEN MELISSA GRADUATED from her Texas high school in 2007, she was excited to go on a mission trip to Mexico later that June. Her church youth group overlapped with her homeschooling circle, so she'd be with kids she'd known since fourth grade. One of her good friends—her best friend, really—was Daniel. Like most of the crowd, he came from a large family. Melissa's family was unusually small (just her, her brother, and parents) but valued similar things: Christian education, character development, and sexual purity. Melissa was on board with all of it. She had resolved to stay a virgin until marriage and was saving her first kiss as a treasure for the right person.

As anticipated, the mission trip was tremendous. Each day surged with adrenaline from the physical activity of working with children. Each evening buzzed with laughter as the group shared silly pranks and language mix-ups. But underneath the laughter flowed the knowledge that they were making a difference in the name of Jesus.

Intoxicated by their shared sense of purpose, Melissa and Daniel talked late into the evenings. In low tones they discussed faith, redemption, and the meaning of life. They divulged their hopes for the future, not only for college and jobs but also for a partner and children. All around them swayed tall Mexican sunflowers whose reddish-orange blooms communicated heat and possibility. As Melissa and Daniel whispered together in the cooling wind, their friendship flowered into romance. It felt inevitable, and perfect, when they kissed. It felt equally inevitable, and equally perfect, when Daniel proposed and Melissa accepted.

In her bones, Melissa knew this was how it should be. No dating, no game-playing, no pawing in the dark. A relationship anchored in years of friendship had deepened through a week of shared service. Melissa didn't need a ring to prove that Daniel was "the one." She locked his proposal in her heart, her own precious secret. They would tell everyone soon enough. But there was another girl back home, and Daniel needed to let her down gently. Melissa understood. Daniel's concern showed the kind of man he was, the partner he would be.

PURITY CULTURE TRAINING: HOMESCHOOLING

Melissa was apprehensive about telling her mother the news. Daniel's family didn't meet Mother's exacting standards. An engagement was a particularly sensitive subject, homeschool's crowning achievement. Mother had invested *years* of effort in this project. If she was unhappy with the result, she was fully capable of making Melissa's life miserable.

Homeschooling had been Father's idea. He was highly educated and wanted his children to receive a top-notch education uncontaminated by secular culture. When he decreed that Mother was to homeschool the two children, she obeyed. Her own upbringing had been marked by "secular teachings" that led to "heartbreak." To her, the rules of homeschool culture offered an alternative, a recipe for happiness—more than a recipe, a talisman to ward off future heartbreak.

The rules were built around this belief: marriage was a sanctified and unbreakable bond between husband and wife. At their wedding, husband and wife were to offer each other their purity, the most important gift a person would ever give or receive. The husband was to be the "head" and the wife was to submit to and fulfill his vision for the family. When they arrived, children would be a blessing from God—more children, more blessing.

Despite her submission to these rules, Mother rarely seemed happy or content. She would say everything was fine when it obviously wasn't. This disconnect bothered Melissa. When Mother was clearly miserable, she would lecture her children about her own traumatic public school experience, as if to convince herself of the need for homeschooling. But if Mother had to do what Father said, why did she rail against it? Yet she did. She begrudged the hours she dedicated to homeschooling, speaking pensively about the imagined career she had sacrificed. Even as a girl, Melissa suspected that her mother chased a phantom of success.

PURITY CULTURE TRAINING: HAIR

Like many daughters, Melissa invested a lot of energy trying to decipher her mother. Since the telephone was her mother's lifeline, Melissa often listened nearby, gleaning information from the one-sided conversations. She gauged the pitch of her mother's voice, the key to reading her mood. Apparently mothers talked about two things: husbands and children. Husband talk was mainly about shared recipes. Children talk ranged more widely, from schoolwork to clothing to dating. But it always circled back to expectations, so different for girls and boys. Occasionally Mother's voice climbed into the highest registers of unhappiness, when she spoke of young people "giving themselves away."

Melissa hated and feared her mother's distress, yet couldn't avoid it. One afternoon when she was five, Melissa cut her own bangs with blunt scissors. Her mother found her in the bathroom with wisps of hair still clinging to the bridge of her nose. Mother snatched the scissors from her daughter and cried, "My life is a disaster! Why do I have to be your mother?" Then she turned the scissors on her own head, hacking great hunks of hair, which fell to the floor. "Am I beautiful now?" she screamed while Melissa cowered.

Another time Mother tried to explain that hair was precious the same way purity was precious, that they were connected, the seen revealing the unseen. People could look at your hair and know what kind of person you were. Melissa's hair might be soft and lustrous now, but when she kissed a boy that would change. The details confused her, but Melissa got the message. Hair wasn't just a woman's badge of beauty. It was her badge of honor or dishonor.

PURITY CULTURE TRAINING: ON THE BEACH

One morning when Melissa was eleven, her mother woke her early. *Dress and get in the car. Just the two of us. A special treat.* As they drove down the highway, her mother cleared her throat and Melissa knew something awful was coming. As the words fell from her mother's mouth—*you're growing up*—Melissa sank into her seat and curled her toes inside her shoes. The words kept falling—*God's design for puberty*—so she curled her toes tighter and tighter, willing the words to stop.

They drove to a diner and ate pancakes and bacon. Then they drove to a beach and walked along the water's edge in bare feet. Melissa's sandy toes ached. Mother talked. "Just know that God has a design for your relationships. Don't give away your purity; it's like giving away your heart. Your purity is the most precious possession you'll ever own."

The shift was too drastic. Bodily topics were normally surrounded by a cone of silence, and Mother had sledgehammered that cone open, all at once. Melissa suspected, rightly, that after this day, the cone would be re-sealed. Still, the idea that God had a design was appealing. Maybe God's design would lead to more happiness than her mother's choices had.

Melissa had no trouble adopting the conservative norms of the homeschool community. For girls, that meant dressing modestly: no short-shorts. No tight tops. No glimpses of bra straps. The courtship model they followed was popularized by Joshua Harris in his 1997 bestselling book, *I Kissed Dating Goodbye*. Instead of dating, which implied fun and friskiness, young people should "court" by forming a relationship that held marriage as the stated goal. The ideal young man and woman would remain sexually pure until their wedding night, abstaining even from kissing.

Some families achieved the enviable gold standard: the young people courted, married their first love, and had children. Even while Melissa sometimes scoffed at the extreme emphasis on purity, she couldn't help but feel moved and inspired by the results. Maybe the teaching was right. Maybe when two people had any sort of sexual contact they gave the other person a piece of their heart. Maybe the happy couples and healthy children were proof that purity paid off.

DAVID AND BATHSHEBA: A FLANNELGRAPH

As a little girl in Sunday school, I loved the flannelgraph lessons. I especially loved David, the shepherd boy who became a king. Or maybe I should say I loved David's sheep, so wooly and white. David wore something like a bathrobe and carried a shepherd's crook. His sheep came in a cluster, the whole flock in one piece. When the teacher stuck them onto the beige, rocky background, I worried they would get thirsty. Fortunately she peeled them off again and put them in a green corner. I knew they needed green pastures and still water. I knew Psalm 23.

When the teacher switched flannel backgrounds from the desert to the city, King David's piece got a fancier robe and a crown. She put him on the palace roof, looking out over the city and whoa!, he saw something. Was that a beautiful woman taking a bath on the roof? The story seemed titillating but also confusing. Why would someone take a bath on the roof? Plus the woman, who was named Bathsheba (get it? Bath/sheba), was taking a bath with clothes on, which made no sense. The teacher said that David fell in love with Bathsheba because she was so extremely beautiful. That part made sense, and it made sense for her to love him back. Who wouldn't fall in love with David, the shepherd boy who killed Goliath?

DAVID AND BATHSHEBA: ALL GROWN UP

Reading the David and Bathsheba story as an adult, I'm struck by the power imbalance between the two characters. King David is not only the most storied man in Hebrew Scripture, he's also the most powerful. His long and complex life is presented in a series of scenes, and he undergoes a constant metamorphosis: David the keeper of sheep transforms into a giant-slayer, a lyre player, Jonathan's BFF, a warrior who kills his ten thousands, the celebrated king of Israel who dances ecstatically before the ark, a hero who defeats an insurrection, and then an old man who requires a beautiful, young virgin in his bed to warm his cold bones. Wielding a shepherd's crook, slingshot, and crown, David is the epitome of the anointed one.

Even so, he's not perfect. Scripture sets the stage for the Bathsheba episode by noting David's neglect of his kingly duties: "In the spring of the year, the time when kings go out to battle . . . David remained at Jerusalem. It happened, late one afternoon, when David rose from his couch and was walking about on the roof of the king's house, that he saw from the roof a woman bathing; the woman was very beautiful." (2 Samuel 11:1-2). It's David who's on a roof, not Bathsheba. Her home is in eyesight of the palace, no doubt because her husband, Uriah, is a general in David's army.

Picture the king on his rooftop, reclining on his royal couch. His troops are endangering their lives to enlarge his property lines, but he'd rather stay in the palace, in safety and comfort. He best lie low. He eats grapes and gets reports from his generals. When he rises to stroll around his roof, he's bored. He restlessly surveys his kingdom, the territory his troops are fighting to extend. He owns all these buildings and properties. The people coming and going are all his vassals.

Then David notices a beautifully dressed woman with her attendants. They're entering the *mikveh*, the ritual bath where she will cleanse herself by dipping in water three times. From his vantage point, David watches her disrobe. She is gorgeous.

> David sent someone to inquire about the woman. It was reported, "This is Bathsheba daughter of Eliam, the wife of Uriah the Hittite." (2 Samuel 11:3)

David knows Bathsheba's husband, Uriah the Hittite. He gives *orders* to Uriah the Hittite!

Never mind that David already has (at least) six wives: Ahinoam, the Jezreelite; Abigail, the Carmelite; Maacah, the daughter of King Talmai of Geshur; Haggith; Abital; and Eglah (1 Chronicles 3). Plus an unknown number of concubines. David desires one more. Not just any one. *This* one. He desires Bathsheba, the wife of Uriah the Hittite.

Knowing she cannot refuse, David summons Bathsheba. We might speculate about the wording and tone of the king's message. Does David assume that a message from the palace will make Bathsheba's heart clutch with fear? After all, her husband is in battle. Does David intensify her worries in order to relieve them? Or does he assume she will welcome his advances? After all, he *is* the king of Israel, her husband's superior.

Scripture does not mention Bathsheba's response. It is irrelevant. When a man has so much power, the woman's acquiescence is assumed. Whatever transpired between the two, the writer did not record it. Bathsheba's thoughts, actions, and words were not worth the papyrus.

What do we call it when a powerful man expects sex from a woman who is not his wife? Some call that adultery. But *adultery* does not connote coercion. When a powerful man forces sex on a woman without consent, that constitutes rape. Could Bathsheba—could any woman—refuse King David? If not, consent is a meaningless concept.

When a man is not only powerful but also respected and charismatic, it becomes almost impossible to say no. Abusers know this and use it to their advantage. Think of men such as Bill Clinton, Bill Cosby, and Bill Hybels. Their power resided, at least in part, in their esteem in the eyes of others. Because of that esteem, these men had the opportunity to prey on multiple women. Just as the #BadBills were each repeat offenders, it seems likely that the same is true of David. Other stories simply went unrecorded. Bathsheba landed in Scripture because the plot spiraled and because her son, Solomon, became king after David. If it were not for those facts, would we know her story?

THE UNEXPECTED: MELISSA

After Melissa said yes to Daniel's proposal, they walked along a Mexico beach. Her mother's warnings about sex could still make her sandy toes cramp, but Melissa felt happy and whole. The magic had happened. A true friendship had blossomed into love. She was reaping the blessing.

A few days after their return, Melissa traveled to north Texas to volunteer as a counselor at a camp for kids in the foster care system. A message was waiting when she arrived. Daniel had been in a skateboard accident, a serious one. He was in the hospital, awaiting emergency brain surgery. Melissa felt shock but put on her happy-Christian mask and went through the motions of helping her group get acquainted.

The next morning, another message arrived. The surgery had not gone well. Could she come immediately? An adult she didn't know drove her home. His kind questions about her "friend" pained her. No one knew Daniel was actually her fiancé. They drove and drove through the heat of Texas scrub country. Melissa prayed silently the way you open a faucet, before you make any attempt to control the flow of water. She poured herself out to God.

As they had so many times over the years, Daniel's family opened their arms to Melissa, Daniel's "best friend." He was on a ventilator and the family wanted Melissa to have the chance to say goodbye. They were waiting to harvest his organs. The phrase devastated her. But even as despair and grief flooded through her, she felt a tinge of duplicity. Daniel's girlfriend, the one he had not yet "let down easy," was also there. Melissa could not breathe a word about Daniel's proposal. Her secret treasure became her secret burden.

Early on Monday morning, exactly one week after he proposed, Daniel died.

THE UNEXPECTED: BATHSHEBA

Second Samuel 11:5 states, "The woman conceived; and she sent and told David, 'I am pregnant.'" Whatever David expected from his dalliance, he may have misjudged Bathsheba. As soon as she misses her period, Bathsheba speaks up. The message she sends to the palace gets right to the point: *I am pregnant.* Scripture records *those* three words.

The pregnancy is a problem. It could ruin David's reputation as a man of God.

When a story is familiar, like this one, the events seem inevitable. Yet they were not. David made the choices he made. To any reader—of Greek dramas, or Shakespeare, or a recent newspaper for that matter—those choices are not surprising. The ancients had a word for excessive pride: *hubris*. In the Greek tragedies, hubris always leads to destruction. The dynamic of devolution is nothing new. We could interpret the #MeToo movement as a response to hubris, an attempt to push back against the overblown pride caused by a too-powerful patriarchy.

David tries to cover his tracks by calling Uriah home from battle. He wants Uriah to have sex with Bathsheba before her pregnancy is discovered. But Uriah is a noble general, mindful of his duty to his men who are camped in battlefields. Uriah refuses the luxuries of his bed and his wife's body.

So David tries again. He summons Uriah to the palace for a nice meal. They eat and drink and discuss the latest troop movements. David makes sure that Uriah gets drunk, hoping to undo the general's scruples. The powerful have always weaponized alcohol. But David has misjudged Uriah too. Instead of going home to have sex with his wife, Uriah bunks with the palace servants.

Thwarted again, David resorts to murder. He writes a message to Joab, the army commander, with instructions to put Uriah on the frontlines, then withdraw military support. What's more, he has Uriah deliver the message. The faithful Uriah hand-carries his execution orders to his executioner.

The next nine verses of 2 Samuel (16-25) supply many details about the fighting—the walls of the city, millstones, arrows, placement of troops. We learn the particulars of how people made war in those days, but the takeaway is simply this: Uriah may have been pierced by the blade of the enemy, the Ammonites, but he perished by the command of his superior, King David.

SILENT NIGHT: MELISSA

Melissa, numb with grief and shock, went through the summer in a trance. In the fall she began attending a community college as she had planned to do. She tried to focus on the subject matter. When Christmas came, the season's festivity sharpened her grief. She and Daniel had always attended the midnight service together. Shoulder to shoulder in a pew, they would share a hymnal even though they knew all the carols. At the end of the service they would pass the light of Christ as the individual flames filled the sanctuary with a holy glow. *Silent night, holy night.* But not this year. Melissa would never again receive the flame from Daniel's lit candlewick to her unlit one.

That Christmas Eve, her parents, as usual, attended an earlier service. Melissa considered inviting John, the boy she had just started to date, to the midnight service, but decided against it. She would hold Daniel's empty place in her heart. She dressed for church as usual, in a black top and plaid skirt. It was cold, so she wore tights and knee high boots.

She found a seat in the rear of the sanctuary, near the end of a pew. The familiarity of the worship service—the poinsettias, the music, the readings—without Daniel's familiar presence became too much to bear. When the candle ritual was about to begin, she was overwhelmed with tears. As the congregation began to sing "Silent Night," Melissa slipped out. Knowing her belongings would be safe, she left her coat and purse on the pew.

Just outside the sanctuary, a hallway connected to the now-dark education wing. Some improvements were underway, so paint fumes and the smell of new carpet assaulted her nose. Melissa didn't care. At least the hallway was blessedly dark. She sank to her knees and sobbed.

It took a moment for Melissa to realize that somebody was beside her, pushing her off-balance. Thinking that someone had tripped over her in the dark, Melissa rocked to the side so they could pass. But instead of moving away, the body slammed hard against her, knocking the air from her lungs. She gasped for air, winded. The body pulled roughly on her legs. She was too stunned and out of breath to move or even make a sound. In that strange silence, she heard, rather than felt, her tights ripping. When she could finally inhale, painfully, she got a lungful of stinking breath. Then the body pinned her down with its weight. It penetrated her and something tore inside of her. The sharp physical pain cut through her psychic numbness.

After he finished and disappeared into the darkness, Melissa lay in the spot where she had first collapsed. Her body was completely cold. She finally moved enough to flap down her wool skirt and felt blood on her fingers. She pulled at her ripped tights and attempted to soak up the blood with the torn fabric. She thought, *My heart is broken, and now my body is too.*

She rolled to her knees, then got to her feet. Footsteps suddenly echoed through the building as people streamed from the sanctuary. Barely ten minutes had elapsed. While the congregation had passed the light of Christ, she had been raped. *Silent night, holy night.* Melissa pushed the thought from her mind. She stumbled against the flow of traffic to the sanctuary to retrieve her coat and purse. None of the joyful worshipers took notice of her. She drove home in silence. This was one more trauma she could never tell anyone.

DAVID MARRIES BATHSHEBA

Second Samuel 11:26-27 states, "When the wife of Uriah heard that her husband was dead, she made lamentation for him. When the mourning was over, David sent and brought her to his house, and she became his wife, and bore him a son." David takes Bathsheba, newly widowed and pregnant, as his wife. Does he love her, or does he feel obligated? What is he trying to redeem—his actions or Bathsheba's place in a society that abandons widows? Whatever David's motives, no doubt the marriage is announced as a noble gesture, evidence of the crown's support for the troops. The royal palace will provide safe harbor to the general's widow with a baby on the way.

No matter how the palace sells the situation to the populace, the Lord is not happy with the king. This chapter ends with these words: "But the thing that David had done displeased the Lord," (2 Samuel 11:27).

It's a curious way to end a chapter, with a comma rather than a period. The punctuation shows that the two 2 Samuel chapters are integrally linked. The question that connects chapters 11 and 12 is this: What, exactly, is David's sin?

WHAT IS DAVID'S SIN?

Notice how Bathsheba is referenced as she changes husbands and homes. Even after Uriah is dead, the writer calls her "the wife of Uriah" (2 Samuel 11:26). This phrase is repeated twice more in the next chapter (2 Samuel 12:10, 15), suggesting that the Lord views Bathsheba as still married to Uriah even after his death and her remarriage to David. This is puzzling. Since the phrase "wife of Uriah" suggests continued possession, or ownership, it may indicate that David's marriage to Bathsheba is a form of theft. If Bathsheba legally belongs to Uriah, and David obtained her through sinful shenanigans, then one of his crimes is that he stole her.

Bathsheba was treated as property that could be stolen because that's what she was. Wives and daughters were chattel, part of a man's holdings, like sheep and goats (it's handy that *chattel* rhymes with *cattle*). To us, the fact that Bathsheba is chattel seems problematic. But in the text the problem is only this: *Whose* chattel is she?

Too often, this story is told ignoring the "women-as-property" prototype that it's based on. But the reader needs to decide whether this prototype is descriptive or normative. In other words, is men-owning-women a social construct of that moment in history (descriptive), or is it God's will for all time (normative)?

If we take the David and Bathsheba story on its own terms, it suggests that a king can own as many women as he wants, as long as he doesn't steal them from one of his generals. But that doesn't preach, does it? Since the story line involves David having sex with Bathsheba, David's sin is often labeled as adultery. But adultery is an odd label for a king who's polygamous and has access to dozens of concubines. What marital bond has he violated? David's targeting of Bathsheba is altogether different from a modern-day husband stepping out on a spouse.

More precisely, what David did with Bathsheba is an abuse of his power. David exploited the enormous power differential that existed between men and women in general, and between himself and any vassal, in order to have sex with a particular woman. The word for that crime is *rape*. When Bathsheba's pregnancy threatened to expose that crime, David attempted a cover up by again abusing his power, this time as commander-in-chief, by sending Uriah to the frontlines unprotected. The word for that crime is *murder*. Both of David's sins were violent crimes rooted in the abuse of power.

When I was a child, David's "downfall" was blamed on Bathsheba's beauty. This is a cunning interpretation. It sidesteps the question of identifying David's sin—adultery, theft, or rape—and simply makes Bathsheba responsible for it. The victim is to blame for being victimized.

This kind of unexamined interpretation does two destructive things. First, it treats rape as equivalent to adultery. But rape is a violent crime while adultery, or misplaced lust, is regarded as the most understandable of all sins. In Dante's *Inferno*, for instance, hell consists of nine concentric circles, deepening toward the pit. Adulterers are in the second circle ("Lust"), just below "Limbo," while violent offenders are much lower, in the seventh circle ("Violence"). Second, blaming the crime on Bathsheba's beauty allows a rapist to blame his sin on the victim—on her beautiful body, her availability. To him, the God-given order of things put her at his disposal.

I wonder if the stranger who raped Melissa grew up hearing Scripture interpreted to make women rape-able.

THE IMBALANCE OF POWER

The paradigm that men are superior to women serves no one. It didn't serve David or Bathsheba, and it doesn't serve us. Men cannot own women. Women belong to themselves in the same way that men belong to themselves. Women have the same intrinsic value as men. Any other paradigm causes suffering.

Even the person in power suffers from having too much power. It's like the adage about being given enough rope to hang oneself. When patriarchal attitudes hand excess power to already-powerful men, it grants them power to destroy—not only those around them but also themselves.

So it happened to David. As king, he had enough power to prey upon others, so he did. He rose—and fell—to that occasion. Somewhere between rising from his couch and strolling across his rooftop, David—the shepherd boy, the giant-slayer, the man of God—became a predator and then a murderer. The transition was seamless, one abuse of power leading to the next. No law or inner compass halted the decline. But God expected him to stop. God expected David's own sense of righteousness to act as a brake.

MELISSA SEEKS COMFORT

The shame and shock of the Christmas Eve rape was too much to contain. Two nights later, Melissa called John, the boy she had just started to date. He came from a similar upbringing and could understand the enormity of this violation. He could help her hold this secret. On the phone, she managed to tell John something of what happened. He expressed shock and immediately offered to come over to comfort her. The allure of confiding her secret was powerful. Melissa warned John she'd have to sneak him into the house and cautioned him to be very quiet. If her parents found him there, they would freak out.

John came over and they quietly sat on the couch in the darkened living room. Melissa swore him to secrecy and choked out her story. She said that if anyone knew, she would never be able to show her face again. John seemed to understand her deep embarrassment. He held her. For a while, she felt safe and warm.

Then John began to kiss her, intently, and she said, "Hold on. Just wait a minute." He pushed and kept pushing. "Just wait a minute!" Melissa, aware that her parents were asleep in the next room, was trying to be quiet. John didn't say anything or make any noise. He didn't have to. He pushed past her *No*. He raped her.

To Melissa's surprise, the penetration hurt again. In that moment, she felt as if her own body had betrayed her. Hadn't the pain the first time been enough? How could things keep getting worse?

Even as John raped her, she knew she could never tell anyone. She knew her parents would say, "I told you so." And maybe they were right. Maybe she deserved this. Maybe she *had* done something shameful. She had sneaked him into the house. She had told him her secret. Who knows? Maybe John was right. He hadn't said it, but he didn't have to. *You're damaged goods. So why not?*

PURITY CULTURE FEEDS RAPE CULTURE

Melissa's story is heartbreaking. It illustrates how the messages of purity culture and rape culture fit together. Both viewpoints treat women as having little agency. Both disregard a woman's bodily integrity. Melissa's first rape on that silent night was a result of rape culture. The second rape, by John, was a result of purity culture. Both rapists treated Melissa as something less than fully human.

To say that the unknown rapist did so for unknown reasons gives him too much credit. We can assume that his "reason" was little more than this: he raped Melissa because he could. She was a woman alone in the dark, unsuspecting and momentarily incapacitated. She was therefore rape-able. This is the simplest indicator of rape culture—that, given the opportunity, it is considered normal for men to rape women. The rapist spotted easy prey. In this scenario, Melissa was "stolen goods."

When Melissa's "friend" John raped her, he was following the logic of purity culture. Even though he originally offered to console her, it seems as though his lens quickly shifted as he realized the implications of what she told him. Since she had been raped, she was no longer virginal and pure but damaged. Her decreased value meant that she was less a person to be in relationship with and more an object to be acted on. She was fair game. In this scenario, Melissa was "spoiled goods."

THE TRAP OF PURITY CULTURE

Purity culture creates a trap. A woman's "most-prized possession" is something that can be ripped from her by force. This implicitly casts women as frail creatures, potential victims, rather than powerful moral agents in their own lives. It downplays their agency. In contrast, purity culture urges men to stay pure, but through a message that has much less intensity. Why are the two genders viewed so differently? Rhetoric about the radically different lives that God intends for women and men is nothing but a smokescreen to hide cultural sins. The two genders were created equal and deserve equal respect and dignity.

How much dignity was involved in Melissa's story? No person should be reduced to just a body or body part. Her physical hymen—flesh that was torn upon penetration—caused bleeding and pain. Repeatedly. Worse, this band of flesh became a metaphor for her inner self. Once her hymen was destroyed, she was destroyed.

In purity culture, the hymen is seen as a gateway to a woman's "pure" core. A woman who "loses" her virginity is regarded with pity or contempt. But virginity is not something a woman can lose in the sense of misplacing it, like a purse. Rather, a woman either chooses to give her virginity to someone, making her a moral agent, or her virginity is taken from her by force, making her a victim. Actual experience might fall somewhere between these two poles, but purity culture doesn't traffic in these realities.

For instance, the concept of consent is intrinsic to sexual activity, yet it is totally absent from purity culture. The emphasis on the submission of a wife to a husband downplays a woman's ability—or need—to exercise agency. If she *must* submit, how can she consent? Paradoxically, a woman is often seen as responsible for her own victimization.

Statistically speaking, a woman's chance of being victimized is one in five.[1] But this reality is not addressed in the teaching of purity culture even though—and here's the kicker—I believe these same teachings *contribute* to victimization. Rather than address these lived realities, purity culture spins a web of abstract gender roles. I suspect that these roles are held dear by people who never owned a hymen.

On a theoretical level, purity culture slots women into one of two roles: a saint or a slut. It's the Madonna/whore complex. A woman is either put on a pedestal as a princess, where she is prized as feminine but sexless, or she is looked down on and feared as a temptress, ascribed neither dignity nor feelings. A saint is a woman without sexual experience, and a slut is a woman who revels in sexual experience. These are opposite ends of a continuum, and neither one is helpful in describing the real life of a woman. And both labels, saint and slut, assume a central tenet of both rape culture and purity culture: that women are somehow responsible for the male gaze.

My flannelgraph Bathsheba story taught me that a woman is responsible for the lust she elicits in a man who ogles her beauty. And also, be beautiful.

THE TRAP OF RAPE CULTURE

Rape culture mandates that women and men have very different sexual responsibilities. The assumption is that it's normal for men to rape women, which means that victims are to blame. By her action (or inaction) a woman creates an opening that allows a man to do what's perfectly natural for him to do—assault her. In this way of thinking, Melissa could be faulted for being alone in the dark, unprotected.

But back away from that just a moment and realize what rape culture is saying: that women are responsible for the actions of men. That women exist in the world as either victims or potential victims because victimization is normative. That men are allowed to take action (with power) and women are acted on (without power), yet women bear the responsibility and pay the price for the actions of men. Note that neither of Melissa's two rapists felt the need to monitor their behavior. Their culture empowered them. Rape culture empowered the Christmas Eve rapist. Purity culture empowered John. The two cultures interlock like shackles.

The power discrepancy between the genders, and the gulf in expectations for behavior, is evident in many places. For instance, they explain the fault lines that appeared when Dr. Christine Blasey Ford testified against Brett Kavanaugh during his Supreme Court justice hearings in September 2018.[2] The testimony of each party was emotional but in different ways, which corresponded with what is allowed according to their gender. Dr. Ford was upset, resolute, and agreeable. She answered every question as completely as possible, showing deference to the members of the Senate Judiciary Hearing committee. In contrast, Judge Kavanaugh was enraged, combative, and tearful. When questioned, he did not answer committee members directly, often insulting the asker. Kavanaugh was allowed to show anger because men are at the top of the pecking order.

What follows from this is important. Although it may seem counterintuitive, powerful men are allowed to posture as victims, a phenomenon captured in the phrase *male fragility*. It was therefore reasonable that the judge would be enraged at having to explain his past behavior. Women, however, must be deferential, even when they have a right to be angry.

BATHSHEBA'S POSTSCRIPT: TAMAR

We've explored Bathsheba's story, told in 2 Samuel 11–12. Chapter 13 continues with the story of Tamar, which was the first story we explored. In many senses, Bathsheba's story gives rise to Tamar's. The characters, plots, and themes overlap.

The two predators are father and son, David and Amnon. The two victims are both women of status who nevertheless cannot control their own fates. Both women are summoned because of their beauty. Both cannot refuse the demands of a member of the royal family.

In both cases the sexual act has consequences that the man does not foresee, although the woman does. Both women raise their voice to force the man to address the consequences of his actions. Tamar does so before the attack, Bathsheba afterward. Tamar anticipates that Amnon will use her and discard her so she delivers a stirring, if unsuccessful, argument to her brother. Bathsheba's initial response to David's summons is not recorded, but she is vocal in notifying the palace when she discovers her pregnancy.

In both stories the crime of rape ultimately leads to bloodshed. In Bathsheba's case, her husband Uriah is murdered by King David as a cover-up. In Tamar's case, her half-brother Amnon, the rapist, is murdered by another brother, Absalom, the heir to the throne, in an act of revenge.

Perhaps the biggest difference between the storylines is the women's ultimate fate. Tamar disappears from Scripture, but Bathsheba gets a happy ending, Bible-style: "Then David consoled his wife Bathsheba, and went to her, and lay with her; and she bore a son, and he named him Solomon. The LORD loved him" (2 Samuel 12:24). What's more, in 1 Kings 1, Bathsheba intercedes with David to ensure that her son Solomon will succeed him on the throne. To have a son become king of Israel is quite a coup. Bathsheba is an unusually clever and resilient woman. But we must also notice that her access to power comes through producing a male child.

Three of these characters—Bathsheba, Solomon, and David—appear in Jesus' lineage: "And David was the father of Solomon by the wife of Uriah" (Matthew 1:6). Technically,

Bathsheba's name does not appear—only her attachment to Uriah—which is an enduring Scriptural reminder that she was stolen and raped. Yet she is named as a foremother of Jesus. It's perhaps an irony of the Davidic line that Jesus' own lineage is steeped in the violation of a vulnerable woman. Rape culture—the normalization of violence against women—is not a new creation but a dynamic that is millennia old, affecting even Jesus' family history.

MELISSA'S POSTSCRIPT

Melissa told me her story a decade after it happened. As we talked, she hemmed a skirt by hand using neat stitches. Melissa had graduated from college, on schedule. Eight years ago, she got married and is now the mother of three. Her interactions with her young children are marked by affection and good humor. When I asked, she said she hasn't decided whether or not she'll homeschool them. Meanwhile, she's studying midwifery. She hopes to work with women who desire a gentle approach to childbirth, perhaps because they've endured sexual trauma.

We talked about the idea of purity that she grew up with. She said, "The Christmas Eve rape destroyed my purity, but it was so bizarre that I almost convinced myself it didn't count. But when it happened twice, the second time with someone I knew and had been interested in, I didn't feel there was any way to go about recovering what I thought was my purity."

Since then, her ideas about sexuality have changed dramatically. To her, bodies are a good thing. Sexual pleasure is a good thing. Bodies are resilient and not easily damaged. But coming to these conclusions took work. She had to go against the programming of her family, church, homeschool, and youth group. She had to reject the notion that purity is something frail and easily taken. She had to reject the idea that she, herself, was irreparably damaged.

As she explained her new way of thinking, I could see her passion and resilience. I told her so. She replied that it took time to find that resilience. At first she had fallen apart. In her words, she "checked out." After the two rapes she acted in completely uncharacteristic ways. Most notably, she began to shoplift. The fact that her father served in law enforcement made this an ironic, perhaps perfect choice. She said with a deadpan delivery, "Side note, if you ever decide to try shoplifting, don't go for Neiman Marcus. Try Old Navy first." How wonderful to laugh together.

Melissa was caught stealing valuable merchandise and charged with a Class B misdemeanor. She spent a night in jail, in a filthy holding cell where bloody Kotex were stuck all over the walls by their adhesive strips. Melissa explained that the surreal experience felt like the bottom of something. She told me, "Now I realize that my shoplifting was an unconscious scream. My inner state was so miserable that my outsides needed to match."

Help came from an unexpected source. Melissa hired a female attorney to defend her in the shoplifting charge. When she spilled out the whole truth, the attorney said, "Because you were honest with me, I'm going to get this erased from your past. I want you to promise me you won't screw up this opportunity. Go on and do something wonderful."

I would like that attorney to know, she has.

THE TEXT ASKS US

1. How did David's power become his downfall?

2. In what way, if any, is Bathsheba culpable? Or is she a victim?

3. What sin displeased God?

MY HOPE

My hope is that the church can become wise about the gender dynamics involved in power and so-called purity and be courageous in confronting those who abuse their power.

CHAPTER SIX

BETRAYAL AND DECEIT

*It's particularly hard to take being stabbed
in the back close to home.*

CATHARINE MACKINNON

But the thing that David had done displeased the LORD,
and the LORD *sent Nathan to David.*

2 SAMUEL 11:27, 12:1

"DO YOU REMEMBER that scene with the old woman in *Titanic*?" Ginni asked me. We were sitting with cups of tea and plates of chicken salad at my kitchen table. For hours we'd been discussing a painful time at Vienna Presbyterian Church (VPC), the enormous, rather conservative church in suburban Washington, DC, where we first met in 2000. Back then I served as interim associate pastor and Ginni was the administrative assistant for the youth program. We've been friends ever since, often socializing with our husbands and children.

"The guys searching the wreckage have this computerized model of how the ship broke in half and sank, remember that?" Ginni asked. "And they show it to the old woman, Rose. And she says, 'Thank you for that fine forensic analysis. . . . Of course, the experience of it was somewhat different.'"[1]

We laughed together, darkly. The *Titanic* metaphor could apply to Vienna Presbyterian. Only a few individuals felt the direct impact of the iceberg—sexual abuse—but some three thousand parishioners were affected as the youth program groaned, shook, and broke apart. The difference between the two stories might be the timeline. While the *Titanic* sank quickly, VPC at first acted as if it could collide with an iceberg and continue on its way. As for forensic commentary, this chapter will draw from three staff members—my friend Ginni Richards, Reverend Peter James, and Sue Kenyon Hamblen, who was also the mother of a victim. They share their perspectives in the hope it will help prevent similar abuse from happening in other churches and, if it does occur, help churches know how to respond.

THE PROPHET NATHAN ENTERS

When 2 Samuel 11 ends, the crisis in the story of David and Bathsheba appears to be over. Uriah is dead. Bathsheba is pregnant. King David has welcomed a new wife into the palace. The last sentence of chapter 11 hangs in mid-air, ending with a comma: "But the thing that David had done displeased the LORD," (2 Samuel 11:27).

The first verse of chapter 12 completes the cliffhanger: "and the LORD sent Nathan to David" (2 Samuel 12:1). Now we understand the reason for the dramatic punctuation. When a prophet pops up at the palace, perk up your ears! Nathan will surely enlighten the king about why the Lord is *displeased*.

HITTING THE ICEBERG

In 2005, the youth group at VPC boomed with some 150 students, from middle school to senior high. Activities ranged from Bible study and overnight retreats to working at a food pantry. In September another busy year was ramping up when rumors crept through church hallways and slithered into the parking lots. Eric DeVries, the youth director, had had an "inappropriate relationship" with one of the girls in the senior high group.

Church members were astounded. Eric was the very model of a young Christian man: good-looking, well-mannered, and deferential. He sang in the choir, literally. The youth ministry program had flourished under his four years of leadership. The idea that he had committed some sort of abuse was upsetting. Many church members refused to believe it.

Reflecting on that revelation some fourteen years later, Ginni said ruefully, "You can 'Monday morning quarterback' all you want, but you see what someone trustworthy wants you to see. If you have a suspicious nature, you might wonder. But there were people at church so enamored of Eric, they wanted their daughters to date him. Young women adoring him. Young men admiring him. Parents who think he's a respectable fellow."

September 2005 was a month Ginni will never forget. Her only child, a son, headed off to college, then a very close family friend died of suicide. She was already feeling shattered when Eric phoned to say, "I didn't want to bother you because you have this other thing going on. But I have to tell you something."

At the time, Ginni assumed that Eric genuinely wanted to spare her from difficult news. But later, she wondered whether he had taken advantage of her. Maybe what felt like friendship was actually manipulation. Predators groom their character witnesses as well as their victims. Eric told her, "I've had an inappropriate relationship with one of the students."

Ginni's reaction was immediate and impulsive: whatever he'd done, Eric was just being stupid. Like the captain of the *Titanic*, Ginni believed what she could see—Eric's goodness. She had no idea there was a mountainous iceberg below the surface, hidden for a reason. And she thought she knew Eric pretty well. When he started at VPC in the fall of 2001, he lived at her home for some months. He was thirty-one years old then, so he came and went as he pleased. Ginni simply extended hospitality, which, as her friend, I know to be her trademark characteristic.

"In retrospect, I suppose he was like Eddie Haskell," she said wryly. "Always flattering, always nice, always, 'Can I be helpful?'" Eddie Haskell was the super-polite kid on the classic TV show *Leave It to Beaver,* always sucking up to his neighbors Ward and June Cleaver. He was a brown-noser and sycophant. Eddie's good manners were meant to distract the Cleavers from whatever mayhem he was causing elsewhere.

THE PROPHET AND THE PET LAMB

The prophet Nathan begins his visit with David by telling a story about a pet lamb. It begins innocently, with endearing details:

> There were two men in a certain city, the one rich and the other poor. The rich man had very many flocks and herds; but the poor man had nothing but one little ewe lamb, which he had bought. He brought it up, and it grew up with him and with his children; it used to eat of his meager fare, and drink from his cup, and lie in his bosom, and it was like a daughter to him. (2 Samuel 12:1-3)

The prophet paints a pleasing picture. The bleating lamb nibbles tidbits from the family's meager table. She drinks water from a shared cup. At night, she nestles her woolly self against the poor man to warm his bones. The beloved lamb is warmth and companionship. She has been *bought*, suggesting the sacrifice a poor family made on her behalf. She is *like a daughter*.

Nathan continues, "Now there came a traveler to the rich man, and he was loath to take one of his own flock or herd to prepare for the wayfarer who had come to him, but he took the poor man's lamb, and prepared that for the guest who had come to him" (2 Samuel 12:4). Like the flash of a knife, the story's tenderness disappears! It's appalling that a rich man would steal from a poor one but to kill and eat a family pet? It's downright beastly.

Hearing the story, David immediately knows who is right and who is wrong. He even knows what punishment is just. Filled with righteous anger, the king proclaims, "As the LORD lives, the man who has done this deserves to die; he shall restore the lamb fourfold, because he did this thing, and because he had no pity" (2 Samuel 12:5-6).

David identifies the sin as theft. Since a rich man robbed a poor one, the king assigns a proportional punishment: "he shall restore the lamb fourfold." This restitution creates justice because it begins to equalize the inequality between the two men. Otherwise the rich man is untouchable—he can afford to pay a penalty while the poor man could never manage court costs. David also seems aware that the rich man's sin is his flagrant abuse of power—"he had no pity." King David dispenses punishment in a breath: "the man deserves to die."

AN ACCUSATION

VPC should be forever grateful to a suspicious younger sister. This fourteen-year-old wondered why the youth director spent so much time in her home—sharing dinner with her family two or three evenings a week and sitting on the couch with her sixteen-year-old sister past eleven at night. In fact, Eric had his own key and came and went at all hours. The parents welcomed his presence, but the younger sister was mistrustful. She began to follow the couple and check their devices. One day in early September 2005, she discovered sexually explicit text messages on her sister's phone, sent by Eric.

The younger sister reported the text messages to a church staff member, who arranged for her to meet with himself and the church's senior pastor, Reverend Peter James. When the two men heard the serious nature of the sister's concerns, they arranged another meeting, this time with the sixteen-year-old victim and Eric. At that confrontational meeting, the victim huddled in a chair and sobbed while Eric admitted that he had crossed boundaries. When they asked if there were any other families they should speak with, Eric mentioned two names.

The next day, James disclosed the bare facts to staff members and cautioned them not to speak about the matter until the session (the church's governing board) had the opportunity to meet the following week. Believing they should investigate the situation themselves, the church staff waited more than two weeks before calling Child Protective Services. During that time they spoke to the parents that Eric mentioned. Both families said they would handle the situation themselves. One of those mothers was Sue Kenyon Hamblen, who overheard people discussing the first victim. Wanting to protect her eighteen-year-old daughter from that gossip, she resisted the severity of the situation. Years would pass before the daughter was ready to disclose the full reality of her relationship with Eric. Meanwhile, CPS was only told about one victim, the first one to surface.

The session met on September 26. The minutes read, "Eric DeVries submitted his resignation, citing inappropriate behavior and sexual misconduct with students as his reason." Years later James regretted that the church forced Eric to resign rather than terminating him. As it was, many church members felt that forcing Eric's resignation was abrupt and unfair.

Conjecture filled the place of facts. How many victims were there? Some accused the victim(s) of being seductive, of making it difficult for Eric to restrain himself. After all, their "logic" went, he was a young, single man surrounded by temptation. Meanwhile the parents of the initial victim heard what had happened under their noses. As they reeled, gossip compounded their sense of betrayal. The Christian community is supposed to offer comfort. When it turns on vulnerable people, the resulting pain is especially acute.

"We're all so much smarter now, thanks to the #MeToo movement," Ginni said over our cups of tea. "But at the time, it was unbelievable that Eric would prey upon the girls under his care." People hesitate to believe the unbelievable. The church members believed Eric was a trustworthy Christian leader. Of course he was! How else could you explain the moving worship services every year on Youth Sunday? Didn't those testimonies reflect the spiritual strength of the youth program?

What I can't help but notice is the ease with which a conservative religious system such as VPC blames the victim. By calling her a temptress, the victim can be recast as the perpetrator.

YOU ARE THE MAN!

While David's words from 2 Samuel 12:5 still hang in the air—the rich man "deserves to die!"—the prophet Nathan delivers his denunciation. Imagine these words coming from a wizened figure like Gandalf in *The Lord of the Rings*, complete with theatric finger-pointing: "'*You* are the man!'" (2 Samuel 12:7, emphasis added).

The simple sentence rings with truth, although it may be hard for us to decipher that truth. The meaning of the phrase has changed over time. Coming from Nathan, "You are the man!" conveyed accusation and condemnation. But in recent years, "You are the man!" conveys approval and even congratulations. The evolution of that phrase is undoubtedly bound up with shifting notions of what it means to be *the man*.

ERIC'S DEPARTURE

Eric's departure from VPC should have been handled with great intentionality. At the time, the church leaders felt they were doing just that. But they didn't access expert counsel as they should have. When they set up a congregational meeting for Eric to make a confession, they felt they exercised control by escorting him in and out of the event and disallowing any interaction with students. But the vague words Eric used to describe his behavior—"inappropriate relationship" and "crossed boundaries"—fell far short of the powerful confession the leaders anticipated. Without intending to do so, they allowed Eric's departure to be shaped by what he failed to say.

Allowing this pseudo public "confession"—however well-intentioned—layered more damage on the victim(s) and created a ring of secondary victims who believed Eric's lies and evasions. For his part, Eric never confessed his sin (and crime). The extent of Eric's abuse needed to be publicly exposed so that other victims, were there any, could come forward. The church leaders should have recognized the likelihood that other victims existed. They should also have worked proactively to provide support and counseling to the victim(s), specifically trauma-informed care (care that takes seriously the neurobiology of trauma).

In their immediate response to the crisis, the leaders also failed to ask a key question: what about the church culture allowed a predator to thrive in secret for four years?

Meanwhile, rumors about lawsuits swirled through the church.

MURDER, THEFT, AND DECEIT

Nathan's accusation rings through the air: "You are the man!" But he is not done. He thunders on, reproaching David for abusing the power God granted him. He makes a verbal heap of all the gifts God piled on David, reminding him that he didn't become king on his own merits: "Thus says the LORD, the God of Israel: I anointed you king over Israel, and I rescued you from the hand of Saul; I gave you your master's house, and your master's wives into your bosom, and gave you the house of Israel and of Judah; and if that had been too little, I would have added as much more" (2 Samuel 12:7-8).

Nathan spells it out: David landed in the palace because the Lord put him there, and now he's forgotten who's in control. Then the prophet names David's sin in three ringing phrases: "You have struck down Uriah the Hittite with the sword, and have taken his wife to be your wife, and have killed him with the sword of the Ammonites" (2 Samuel 12:9).

Three phrases for three sins: murder, theft, and deceit. Murder, because David sent Uriah to the battle frontline unsupported—he might just as well have wielded the deadly sword himself. Theft, because David took Uriah's wife to be his own, stealing the dead man's property. Deceit, because David's trickery in killing Uriah did not fool the Lord. In fact, David's attempt to disguise his actions only intensified the Lord's displeasure.

For contemporary readers, two of David's three sins are clear enough: murder and deceit. But we may balk at the sin of *theft*. The "stolen object" is a *person*, someone's wife. Can a woman actually be stolen, like a necklace or laptop? She isn't a possession. She's a human being with dignity, belonging not to another person but to God.

Yet the text repeatedly implies that David stole Bathsheba from Uriah. Nathan refers to Bathsheba as the "*wife* of Uriah the Hittite" even after his death, three times. *Widow* is a common Hebrew word, so why doesn't Nathan use it? Even the genealogy of Jesus in the Gospel of Matthew, written centuries later, mentions Bathsheba as "the wife of Uriah" (Matthew 1:6).

Nathan's story also highlights David's sin of theft, with the poor man's pet lamb functioning as a stand-in for Bathsheba. Nathan mentions the lamb's gender twice in just a few sentences: the "ewe lamb" is like a "daughter" (2 Samuel 12:3). *Daughter is* a surprising word to use for an animal, even a pet. If the lamb represents Bathsheba, the word *daughter* underscores the difference in how the two men treat the lamb: a *beloved* versus an *object*.

The rich man had not just one beloved lamb but "very many flocks and herds" (2 Samuel 12:2). Nathan is alluding to David's numerous wives and concubines. The king's harem was a status symbol that carried practical benefits. At least some of David's marriages cemented international alliances—notice how his first three wives are designated: Ahinoam the Jezreelite, Abigail the Carmelite, Maacah the daughter of King Talmai of Geshur (see 1 Chronicles 3:1-2). The plethora of wives also insured an abundance of descendants to carry on the royal name and lineage. Whether or not the king loved the women wasn't a primary concern. The wives had utility, like "flocks and herds."

In contrast, Uriah had a single wife, Bathsheba, "one little ewe lamb." Although the earlier chapter didn't indicate that Uriah and Bathsheba were a particularly devoted couple, Nathan's metaphor suggests that this was the case. That the ewe lamb is unable to speak hints that Bathsheba was unable to protest David's actions. She was rendered mute by the power differential between herself and the king. The language of "little ewe lamb" may also suggest youthfulness. Bathsheba is likely in her twenties, while David is fully mature, in his fifties. The whole metaphor raises the issue of consent. Due to stark disparities in status, power, and age, was meaningful consent possible in the story of David and Bathsheba?

To state the obvious, similar questions of consent apply to a youth director in his early thirties who preys on teenagers he is responsible for. The stories at VPC illustrate how age can muddy issues around consent. If a girl has been groomed for a period of years, does turning eighteen make her able to freely decide to "date" her predator?

GINNI CAMPAIGNS FOR ERIC

When word came that one of the victims was filing charges against Eric, Ginni wanted to be sure he got a fair shake. To her mind, he was innocent until proven guilty. As the administrative assistant for the youth group, Ginni wrote an email to approximately thirty families and volunteers who were heavily involved in youth activities. Before she sent the email, she got permission from her boss. It read, "Dear Friends, I am writing to you in the hope that you would consider sending a letter of support on behalf of Eric DeVries. . . . In the letter describe you or your family's relationship with Eric. Comment on his character and your experience with him."

That action would torment Ginni in the months to come. In fact, writing that email is the single biggest regret of her life. She teared up as she wondered aloud whether her action prevented victims from coming forward. "My bent, for right or wrong, is to be helpful. But I wasn't. I should have stepped back and let it play out." At the time, she thought the letters would provide "balance" to the judge. Now she realizes that balance is an inappropriate concept for sexual abuse. No good act cancels out abusive acts. She also clearly sees that she functioned as part of the system to minimize Eric's abusive behavior.

Knowing Ginni, I glimpse the dynamics at work. She didn't intend to hide or excuse a predator, although that was the effect of her actions. At that point she was unwilling to believe he *was* a predator. She couldn't align the disjointed rumors she heard with the Eric she thought she knew. Maybe she resisted the truth because she had worked alongside him for years. Maybe she resisted because he vigorously maintained his innocence. Maybe the traumatic coincidence of her dear friend's death by suicide numbed her thought process. Undoubtedly, Ginni was swayed by a factor that influenced so many others. Her own son, now in college, had previously had a positive relationship with Eric. She didn't want to let go of something seemingly solid in the midst of so much slipperiness.

Letters of support poured in, twenty-five in all. One mother stopped Ginni in the stairwell and said, "I don't need to know and I don't want to know, I just want to tell you that my son is devastated by all this because he really thought Eric was a good guy." That seemed to sum up the thoughts of many people. They resisted the knowledge that they had been deceived and betrayed.

Someone forwarded Ginni's email to the mother of one of the victims, who became incensed. That mother confronted Ginni, a day she will never forget. "I rightly got my ears boxed," she told me. "I felt terrible. I didn't understand the depth and complication of their situation."

For his part, Eric never told Ginni the truth—not even in confidence.

NATHAN'S JUDGMENT

There will be hell to pay. Nathan pronounces judgment on David.

> Now therefore the sword shall never depart from your house, for you have despised me, and have taken the wife of Uriah the Hittite to be your wife. Thus says the LORD: I will raise up trouble against you from within your own house; and I will take your wives before your eyes, and give them to your neighbor, and he shall lie with your wives in the sight of this very sun. (2 Samuel 12:10-11)

David sinned by robbing Uriah of his wife, so in repayment the Lord will take away David's wives and give them to a neighbor. It's disturbing to read about women being treated like property, passed around tit for tat. That the Lord decrees such a thing is something to be reckoned with.

Still, Nathan's message contains an unexpected sort of liberation for survivors of sexual assault. The good news lodges in what he *doesn't* say: by naming David's sin as theft, he doesn't name it as sexual sin, the paradigm commonly applied to Bathsheba's story. But Nathan implicitly says, forget the focus on "adultery." Forget the suggestion that Bathsheba "seduced" David by disrobing on a roof. Forget the Sunday school rendition of an epic love story between a handsome king and a willing woman.

Nathan frames David's sin as theft, articulating an often overlooked truth: in sexual violation, the abuser steals from the victim. We can count the host of losses suffered by Bathsheba, all directly flowing from her abuse. She loses her husband. She loses her child. In a very real sense, she loses her future, or at least the version of the future in which she bears children to Uriah and grows old with him. That future was stolen from her.

Similarly, the members at VPC lost many things—some of which they did not recognize for years.

ERIC'S ARRAIGNMENT

After he resigned, Eric moved back to his hometown in the Chicago suburbs. Some church members assisted him with the logistics of moving, which infuriated other members. When he flew back to Virginia in December for his arraignment, Ginni agreed to drive him from the airport to the courthouse.

I asked her why she did that. She shrugged her shoulders. "He needed to appear before the court, and he needed a ride," she said.

The judge read the two charges against Eric: taking indecent liberties with a minor (a felony that requires registry as a sex offender) and contributing to the delinquency of a minor (a lesser charge). Ginni watched numbly as the officers remanded Eric into custody. Through a doorway, she glimpsed an orange jumpsuit. That color spoke louder than any words. This was a place for criminals.

Eric spent the night in jail, and Ginni picked him up the next morning. She waited while he posted bail and received his court date. She didn't know, and didn't want to know, how he got bail money. Sitting in the waiting room, she felt like a criminal herself. She prayed for wisdom and courage.

As they pulled away from the courthouse, Eric defended himself to Ginni, "You know [a girl from youth group] came on to me."

As Ginni recounted this story to me, she became angry all over again: "I'm thinking, why are you blaming this girl? Who was the *adult* in the room?" She sat up straight at my kitchen table and turned in her seat to punch an imaginary Eric with her fist.

"Did you really hit him?" I asked, surprised.

"I did. I remember my fist bouncing off his coat," she answered. "I yelled, 'What the hell is wrong with you?'"

NATHAN THE ENFORCER

It is exceedingly rare for an abuser to admit sin. It speaks to David's character that he did so. When Nathan condemns him ("You are the man!"), David responds, "I have sinned against the LORD" (2 Samuel 12: 7, 13).

While we might wish that he included "and against Bathsheba," David appears to be humbled. He recognizes that he has abused his power and prerogative. What's more, he himself has named the stakes for this sin: he deserves to die.

Only a tiny fraction of abusers ever admit fault. As an attorney once told me, abusers are notoriously "immune to insight." Since most abusers never admit guilt, the next steps become impossible: repentance, restitution, and reconciliation. Churches must face the sobering reality that while they can denounce an abuser—"You are the man!"—the abuser is likely to ignore the indictment. Apparently the temptation to rationalize one's sins and crimes is such a Goliath that it takes someone of David's stature—a giant-slayer—to admit guilt.

ERIC REFUSES TO ADMIT GUILT

Before returning to Chicago, Eric stopped by Ginni's house to pick up some items. They stood in her cozy family room, the scene of so many conversations over the past four years, especially during the months he had lived in her home.

She said, "Eric, everyone is saying you're a sexual predator."

He reared back as if she hit him. But this time his face contorted and the mask slipped. In that moment she saw the truth of who he was.

Ginni told him, "You need help." It was their last conversation before he flew back to the Midwest.

PROPHET AS LAW ENFORCER

As a prophet, Nathan's role is similar to that of modern police officers. Positioned outside the everyday arena, his words carry great weight and authority. Perhaps this is one reason David can hear Nathan's indictment. The prophet speaks for the Lord, a voice not easily ignored. Such high authority can bestow heavy punishment. You might say the Lord's authority is not only eternal but also external. If churches want to follow Nathan's method with abusers, they must turn to external authorities such as law enforcement. No other method will bring abusers to account. They are too adept at deceit.

Nathan, a prophet and enforcer, a spokesperson for God, explains the recompense that the Lord has assigned: "'Now the LORD has put away your sin; you shall not die. Nevertheless, because by this deed you have utterly scorned the LORD, the child that is born to you shall die'" (2 Samuel 12:13-14).

Even though David admits his guilt and the Lord *put away* the sin, the Lord does not put away the punishment. An innocent one will suffer for David's sin.

PUNISHMENT FOR ERIC

When Eric flew back to northern Virginia for his court date in February 2006, Ginni again gave him a ride. The day was cold, with a bright blue sky. They parked at his lawyer's office to walk to the nearby courthouse. As they got close, Ginni saw the family members of one of the victims standing outside and instantly felt sick to her stomach. What if they saw her and thought she was protecting Eric? That's not what she was doing, was it? Her heart pounded and she couldn't breathe. She wanted to flee. Was it right to abandon a former friend? Following her impulse, she turned on her heel and walked back to the lawyer's office.

Later, Eric told her what happened in court. He pleaded guilty to the lesser offense of "contributing to the delinquency of a minor." A *minor*, singular. Even though he abused multiple girls at VPC, only one family had filed charges. Since it was his first offense, he received a suspended sentence. No parole. No ankle bracelet. No registry as a sex offender.

After he returned to Chicago, Eric called Ginni twice. The first time, he sounded like a kid with a good report card. "Guess what my counselor said? That I'm better than most." He wanted her to believe he'd been healed. She hung up. She would not be deceived again. A second phone call came out of the blue saying he missed her. On her end, Ginni simply wondered what he wanted. Whatever it was, she wasn't about to give it to him.

PUNISHMENT FOR DAVID

David and Bathsheba's child grows sick, and for a week, fights to live. David prostrates himself on the floor and fasts. His behavior is the exemplar of penitence. It scares the servants, who fear what the king might do if the child dies. "David therefore pleaded with God for the child; David fasted, and went in and lay all night on the ground. The elders of his house stood beside him, urging him to rise from the ground; but he would not, nor did he eat food with them. On the seventh day the child died" (2 Samuel 12:16-18).

How fascinating that David pleads and fasts for this baby's life. After all, with seven wives it's unlikely there's a shortage of palace babies. Opportunities abound to make more. So why is he invested in this particular child? It could be a sign that he especially loves Bathsheba.

Or—more likely—a keen sense of guilt drives David to the floor. His act of prostration becomes an act of atonement. As the hours and days pass, the humble posture engenders a humble spirit. He has ample time to contemplate his life and legacy. At his age, more life lies behind him than ahead. What has he done with his years? His penitence becomes his reckoning.

If David's response were typical of abusers, the #MeToo movement would not need to exist.

THE RECKONING

When the child dies, David gets up from the floor, bathes, puts on fresh clothes, worships at the temple, and sits down to a meal. This odd behavior puzzles the servants. When they ask David his reasoning, the answer is poignant: "Can I bring him back again? I shall go to him, but he will not return to me" (2 Samuel 12:23). Those words surely resonate with anyone who has grieved the finality of a loved one's death. They ring with a different kind of finality for the lifelong changes in a victim of sexual abuse.

The whole of 2 Samuel 12 is concerned with David's internal state, but he is not the only one to suffer in this chapter. A mother has prayed for healing, then grieved the death of her newborn. A blameless infant has died. These other points of view—mother and child—appear only between the lines. They are insignificant to the writer, who conveys the entire Bathsheba story as a leitmotif in the larger arc about David, the Great Man. We readers must bring the invisible victims to light.

While it's disheartening that Bathsheba is a bit player in her own story, David's penitence holds out hope. If redemption is available to a man as powerful and abusive as David, it is available to any abuser. David sinned greatly, but he also heard Nathan's ringing judgment, confessed, and accepted his punishment. Very few abusers follow this lead.

What if Eric had acknowledged his sin? What if he confessed before God and the community that he manhandled precious "ewe lambs"? What if he acknowledged his manipulation, trickery, secrecy, and abusive behavior? What if he had paid an appropriate punishment for his crime? As it was, a congregation of more than three thousand believers suffered because of Eric's betrayal and deception.

THE HEALING CIRCLE

In the fall of 2008 a new associate pastor, the Reverend David Jordan-Haas, came to VPC. He heard stories about the sexual, emotional, and spiritual abuse that Eric inflicted for more than four years. Even though other leaders felt that the problem—now three years in the past—was largely resolved, Jordan-Haas recognized how it continued to affect the church in profound but hidden ways.

In March of 2009, the parents of one of the victims initiated a healing circle for the victims, parents, and church leaders, about a dozen persons in all. The parents hired facilitators and counselors who led the event based on a therapeutic model. The healing circle was held in a local high school because one of the victims became traumatized at the thought of entering the church building.

That afternoon, Ginni had the opportunity to explain about the timing of her friend's death and how profoundly it affected her. She didn't say this in self-defense but to give context for her actions. She apologized profusely for sending the email that solicited testimonials about Eric's work at VPC. Weeping, she told the girls and their parents that she regretted her actions and would take them back if she could.

Telling me about it years later, she became emotional once again. "I dissolved into a puddle on the floor that day. It was just really, really hard," she said.

The day after the healing circle, Reverend Peter James stopped by Ginni's desk and said with appreciation, "I don't know how you did that." Ginni felt flummoxed at what seemed like a compliment. What had she done? She had become emotional. But she also recognized the tremendous energy she spent in processing these events. Not everyone could, or would, do as she did.

Ginni was grateful for the healing circle. The angry mom—the one who initially confronted her about the email—was gracious after Ginni apologized. From what the victims shared, it was obvious that much of their pain came from the church's response and lack of support.

A participant asked one of the victims, "Is it too late to make things right?"

The girl said, "No, it's not too late."

What a relief to hear that!

"But then we *didn't* make things right," Ginni told me, shaking her head. "We could have done more."

For instance, Ginni suspects that some families at the core of the trauma never received a personal apology from church leaders. And then there's the matter of a fund to pay for ongoing counseling for victims. That promised fund became a sore point because it wasn't handled transparently. The church's 2011 budget reflected zero dollars in the line item for counseling. A staff member assured the victims that money was still available, and always would be, but the amount was hidden to protect their anonymity. Three victims who were now adults didn't accept those reassurances. Besides, they were ready to out themselves. They filed a lawsuit against the church and the case was settled out of court. A court-ordered counseling fund now guarantees coverage for victims for forty-five years, and for family members (parents and siblings) for ten years.

When a church is handling the aftermath of sexual abuse, there can be tension between protecting a victim's identity and providing for her (or his) needs. But it's also easy, and unfortunately common, for churches to claim they're protecting the victim when they're actually protecting their own reputation. Anonymity is not the only, or necessarily best, option.

THE 2011 RECKONING

In 2011, the *Washington Post* ran a five-thousand-word investigative article titled "Vienna Presbyterian Church Seeks Forgiveness, Redemption in Wake of Abuse Scandal."[2] Staff members at VPC—including the three featured here, Ginni Richards, Reverend Peter James, and Sue Kenyon Hamblen—cooperated fully with reporter Josh White. Much of what the explosive article exposed had lain underground in bits and pieces for six years. Ginni, who worked in the very heart of the youth program, had not been privy to much of the information disclosed in the article. Even James, who spent many hours with the reporter, was surprised by some of the material unearthed.

VPC's experience is a striking example of the positive role that investigative journalism can play as churches deal with the aftermath of sexual abuse. Journalists' role has been key since the beginning of the #MeToo movement, and the scope and significance of that role is growing, rather than diminishing. Christians must learn to embrace media coverage as a gift.

Sometimes a painful gift. But the gospel is clear: "Take no part in the unfruitful works of darkness, but instead expose them. For it is shameful even to mention what such people do secretly; but everything exposed by the light becomes visible, for everything that becomes visible is light" (Ephesians 5:11-14).

The facts exposed were shocking. Eric had preyed on *many* girls. He groomed them using his access through the youth program. Stealing moments alone in the church office, the church van, or on retreats and mission trips, he would pray aloud with them and cuddle. The relationships were not only physical but also emotional and deeply spiritual. Each action built to a crescendo carefully timed to the victim's age.

It's no coincidence that Eric orchestrated a full-on Valentine's Day seduction with one victim just as she turned eighteen. When she went off to college, the two began a relationship that was semi-open. Despite the fact that Eric was roughly twice the woman's age, some church members approved of the relationship.

Most of the victims were very young and entirely naive. Eric told at least three girls (and possibly five or more) that he intended to marry her when she became old enough. To one, he read aloud from Genesis 29:18, where Jacob promises to wait seven years to marry his beloved Rachel. A master at praying in a low, husky voice, Eric convinced each one that God willed for them to be together. Someday. For now, only the two of them could know. Isolated and deceived, each girl believed herself to be the chosen one.

These primary targets were not Eric's only victims. At least a dozen girls experienced his inappropriate attentions over the years. In describing their relationships with Eric, many said they felt "under a spell." Because each relationship was highly secretive and laced with God-talk, the abuse was particularly potent and egregious. The combination of sexual and spiritual abuse up-ends a victim's sense of who and what is trustworthy. If a "man of God" is not honorable, does that mean God is not honorable? If having faith in God leads a person into harm, does that mean God desires harm? Violations by faith leaders steal a person's innocent faith and can cause ripple effects for a lifetime.

Eric didn't directly prey on the boys, but they were also victims. Ginni wondered aloud to me, "What did they [the teen boys at VPC] glean about the ways a man should treat a woman? Did they understand where Eric crossed the line and why that was destructive? Were their parents able to process these dynamics with them?" Some parents can have such conversations, others cannot. The church should have exercised leadership in unpacking the aftermath.

In addition, siblings, parents, and the church at large were affected. Much of this collateral damage wasn't apparent for years. It wasn't until after the *Washington Post* article that one VPC staff member was asked to resign.[3]

In hindsight, Ginni wonders about how the church could have handled things more effectively—both in prevention and response. Like other church members, she put implicit trust in the committee that hired Eric. They were impressed that he graduated from Calvin College, a well-respected conservative college.[4] That credential caused a halo effect. But it turned out that a previous church that employed Eric had heard hints of similar abuses. Shouldn't those hints have been verbalized? When does the "right to privacy" function as a screen to pass along a problem? Of course, organizations are wary of liability.

In the absence of an actual conviction, they're hesitant to comment on a person's ethical behavior. But concern for liability can undermine the body of Christ.

Ginni was incensed to discover that one of Eric's previous employers (a Christian summer camp) had contacted James about some "inappropriate" behavior the summer before he began at VPC. There were two incidents, both minor, but prohibited behaviors. In one, he was alone with a camper, and in the other, he sent an innocuous text message. These minor trespasses are exactly the kind of behaviors that perpetrators typically use to gauge an organization's response to boundary-crossing. How carefully are rules upheld? Imagine the suffering the church could have avoided if his actions had been more thoroughly investigated and addressed. As it was, VPC mandated that Eric receive counseling, but he snowed the counselor with deceit.

Ginni also dared to voice other, disturbing questions: "Was Eric drawn to work with youth in churches because he had easy access to targets? Did he have a spiritual hunger? Where does sinfulness end and mental illness begin?"

What Ginni doesn't ask, but I do, is this: In what ways did the church's conservative culture prepare a seedbed for abuse to go underground? When homosexuality is a taboo subject, when abstinence is the assumed "right answer" for any teen question about sex, when norms around modesty are held especially dear—is it easier for a predator to groom victims?

WHAT WAS STOLEN

The Nathan story frames David's sin as theft. If we were to ask the victims at VPC what was stolen from them, they would probably name all sorts of precious things, like their belief that the world is trustworthy or a lighthearted sense of safety, wholeness, and joy.

Even the secondary victims—the girls, boys, women, and men who were peripheral to Eric's abuse—lost things. They lost their confidence in the security and safety of their faith community. They lost innocence. Their trust in God's unshakable Word was shaken because a faith leader twisted verses to manipulate the vulnerable. In a very real sense Eric stole the past—formerly happy memories are forever tainted by the revelation of what really went on. He also stole the future—the youth program may never have the vigor it once enjoyed. Most people at VPC are reluctant to say the name of Eric DeVries aloud.

Some of Eric's victims may even relate to the chilling image in Nathan's story, the ewe lamb on a platter, slaughtered for the enjoyment of the rich man and his guest. As we saw in Melissa's story, some survivors have experienced their very flesh ripping to satisfy male appetites.

While the paradigm of theft may not at first seem adequate for the sin of sexual abuse, it is surprisingly helpful. Too often—at least in Christian communities—sexual abuse is regarded as a private sexual sin. In the eyes of many, sexual sin is especially understandable. No doubt this is why abusers are often allowed to make secret confession and absolution while justice for the (usually female) victim goes unaddressed. Even worse, the discrepancy in how the genders are regarded heaps shame on a female victim whose sexual purity has been damaged. Nathan's focus on theft presents a powerful alternative to this purity/shame narrative. Every culture knows how to punish a thief whose actions damage an entire community. It's the very reason legal systems were created.

A PASTOR'S PERSPECTIVE

James told me that the magnitude of what happened struck him years after the fact, when one of the former youth asked to meet with him. She told a story that pierced him, perhaps because it came from the fringe of the abuse and showed the extent to which Eric's behavior had permeated the church. James said, "A student not identified in the original abuse asked to meet with me. She told a similar story of being prepared for sexual exploit. One afternoon, Eric made his advance and she bolted. It dawned on me as she shared her story. We had a sexual predator on our staff and no one knew a thing about it, except for his victims."

James hopes that other churches will learn from VPC's experience. With the benefit of hindsight, he acknowledges that the church failed to access expert assistance when the crisis broke. He also readily agrees that the church should have demonstrated more remorse, more quickly. He acknowledges the forces pushing against public disclosure. External forces—insurance professionals—urged him not to make a public apology for reasons of liability. By making the compelling case that caution would safeguard the church's financial future, they made silence seem prudent. Besides those external forces, James acknowledges that internal forces urged him to "move on." This was an ugly chapter in his long history with the church, a chapter he was eager to close. So VPC did what churches are tempted to do in the aftermath of trauma—it moved on too soon.

Speaking as someone who once worked on the pastoral staff at VPC, and as someone who respects James, I suggest that he—and most pastors—need to reframe their understanding of their pastoral role after abuse. Pastors are accustomed to thinking of themselves as leaders. In the face of crisis, that translates to damage control—when a destructive narrative surfaces, leaders reshape it to cause as little damage as possible. But after abuse, a pastor must work in the opposite direction to more fully excavate and expose the destructive narrative. This advocacy work can be counterintuitive to a leader. But when abuse surfaces, pastors must lead differently—by becoming advocates for the vulnerable.

On the Sunday before the *Washington Post* story appeared, James broke from the advice of his insurance company and boldly offered a public apology during worship. He agonized over his words. They all seemed inadequate. In the end, he said, "How deeply I regret what happened to you. I apologize for what has occurred. It happened on my watch, and I am sickened by the devastation it has caused. Some of our survivors feel under-supported by this church and me in particular. I am truly sorry."

Although there are other things he might do differently, he never regretted the decision to offer that public apology.

A MOTHER'S PERSPECTIVE

Sue Kenyon Hamblen, the mother of one of the victims, was on staff at VPC at the time. It's a credit to both her and the church that her employment lasted through this ordeal and continues to this day. Sue poured out her heart in a powerful letter that was distributed to the congregation in June 2011, two months after the *Washington Post* article. Since it's common for the families of victims to lose their faith community, I want to lift up the fact that the Hamblens and VPC *refused* to lose each other. It seems fitting to give Sue the last word:

> These have been the most difficult years of our lives. We watched our bright hopeful young daughters become secretive, deceptive, depressed and in some cases self-destructive young adults, all without knowing why. The survivors of Eric's systematic abuse that we can now identify were intelligent, outgoing leaders, athletes and scholars. Their parents, grandparents, siblings and friends were deeply affected by what happened. We've cried buckets of tears, spent countless sleepless nights worrying, devoted endless hours in prayer, and thousands of dollars in therapy and hospitalization costs. Our feelings have see-sawed between rage and anger to sorrow and despair. We're now just beginning to feel hope as VPC (both community and staff) start to recognize and accept the role that they played in this most painful period in our daughters' lives. Some of them will recover and, sadly, others might not. We may never know all of the survivors, and we will surely never know the true impact on each of them.
>
> Now that they are bravely ready to tell their story, we are pleading with all of you to react in a way that will contribute to their recovery. Please don't ask or state the following:
>
> # Why are the girls stirring the pot again
>
> # Why can't we just move on—it's been years
>
> # Well, if they'd told the truth in the first place, we wouldn't be dealing with this now

⌗ The staff made innocent mistakes and now the
girls are causing them to be in trouble

All of these are statements that I've recently heard.

When Eric resigned his position and addressed the two
youth groups and their parents, he lied. He appeared repentant, sad and strangely honorable to some. Some
members of this congregation rallied to his support—
gifts of food, money, letters of reference, prayer circles,
assistance in packing for his move away from here were
all given to Eric. The anonymous victim was often not
kindly spoken of. Given this climate, what shattered ado-
lescent would raise their hand to volunteer their involvement? In truth, some did, but were ignored or not
encouraged. Sexual abuse survivors often can't tell their
stories, but this particular set of circumstances with the
community made it all but impossible.

There may be some of you that wonder if this is the
right church for your family at this time. We considered
finding a new church, and although our daughter worships elsewhere, we have kept this as our church home
and plan to continue. We've long hoped for a healthy,
reconciled, safe and awake church that will overcome the
pain and restore our faith. It is not wrong to love and
support this church through this painful chapter, while
still calling for accountability. Each must decide for
themselves, but we intend to be part of the solution. VPC
has the ability to serve as a beacon of hope when we
truthfully share what we did wrong and how we can help
others prevent, identify, and stop the predators that
desire our children.

Our families have neither issued ultimatums nor made demands. What we did issue was a heartfelt request to seek the truth, acknowledge the pain our girls have endured, and commit to the necessary care they need to heal. These requests have been met. VPC leadership will decide how best to ensure that this never happen again. At this point, all we want to do is concentrate on taking care of our daughters and families.

It is Eric's responsibility to answer to God. We're not interested in vengeance, but we are very interested in stopping him cold. Experts have shared that there is a very high probability that Eric is back in business. Child molesters don't recover, and Eric was neither substantially punished nor remotely rehabilitated. The moral obligation to try to stop Eric is weighty on the girls and we support them wholeheartedly in these efforts. No woman, girl or family should suffer again at the hands of Eric DeVries, and now that we're clear about what he did, none of us should be content until we do what we can to stop him.

Please pray for our families—we need the support and Christian love of this community to facilitate the healing.[5]

THE TEXT ASKS US

1. Who is your Nathan, and do you hear the hard truths he tells you?

2. What do you do when confronted with a hard truth? Are you able to be penitent, as David was?

3. Are there places where you see injustice and could speak the hard truth?

MY HOPE

My hope is that the church can hear a prophetic word and be convicted of its wrongdoing before more vulnerable ones are sacrificed.

CHAPTER SEVEN

VULNERABILITY AND VOICE

*It took me quite a long time to develop a voice, and
now that I have it, I am not going to be silent.*

MADELEINE ALBRIGHT

*Why should the name of our father be taken away
from his clan because he had no son? Give to us
a possession among our father's brothers.*

NUMBERS 27:4

ONCE I BEGAN WRITING about abuse within faith communities, many people reached out to me with stories. One of these was a clergywoman I'll call Stephanie Green. Reverend Green was the associate pastor of a large congregational church in the Chicago suburbs. Over breakfast one Monday morning, she noticed her church's name in the local newspaper. The snippet was posted in the Police Blotter section, the exposed underbelly of suburban life: "Man Banned from Church." Even before she read it, Stephanie knew what the item would say. Her heart sank.

Banned was not a word she would choose to link with her church. The congregation she served was welcoming and full of kindness. It ran a soup kitchen, for heaven's sake! *Banned* was such a weighty word, a word of last resort. Still, it was true, and there it was in print. Someone had indeed been evicted from the sanctuary yesterday. Remembering the incident made Stephanie sad all over again.

At the same time, the memory made her feel strangely calm and centered. When she had expressed her feelings of vulnerability and alarm, the senior pastor had called the police. Officers responded with prompt action because Stephanie's physical and emotional well-being mattered. For her, the sanctuary would continue to be a safe place. She recognized that many women don't have sympathetic colleagues and responsive police officers. Many women don't feel protected. Many are *not* protected. Stephanie felt grateful that she was, and recognized her privilege.

As she tried to sort out her two opposite reactions—dismay and gratitude—Stephanie read the news snippet over and over. The blackness of the typeface and the article's placement on the page imprinted onto her memory. To her, the story symbolized the best and worst of ministry, simultaneously. But as she re-read the item, something unspoken needled her.

THE INCIDENT

That previous Sunday, Stephanie had popped into the sanctuary early, around eight o'clock, to check on the placement of the poinsettias. She would be baptizing an infant during the ten o'clock service, and the cheerful, red-leaved plants that lined the chancel steps created an obstacle course. She wanted to rehearse her footwork.

Pretending to hold a baby in her arms, she turned from the baptismal font—and felt eyes following her. Someone was sitting in the front pew, watching her every move. When Stephanie recognized who it was, she felt prickles of alarm. William was one of the homeless men who frequented the church's soup kitchen. Or rather, he *had* frequented the soup kitchen until two weeks prior when the church leaders asked him to leave the premises and not return.

The trouble had begun innocently enough, months earlier. As part of her routine, Stephanie often chatted with the men while they waited for their meals. William developed something like a crush on her. He began seeking her out in her office, or wherever she might be, even though the soup kitchen had its own dedicated space and the rest of the building was kept separate and locked. William was always able to find her. Even though he appeared to be harmless, Stephanie felt rattled by these dogged attentions.

Compared to many of the rowdy regulars, William was a teddy bear. Tall and broad, with light brown skin, his soft features might have indicated a disability. His long, unkempt hair was straight and dark. No one knew anything about his background. English wasn't his first language, but he wasn't fluent in Spanish either.

Stephanie's fear had escalated when she realized that William followed her when she left the building to grab coffee with a colleague. As she walked back to the church alone, William appeared out of nowhere, trailing her, and calling out, "Why were you walking with that other man when *I'm* your boyfriend?" When she got back to the church she found multiple voicemail messages from William, each one longer and more intense.

Stephanie told the senior pastor about the incident, who encouraged her to report it to the police. She did so, saying,

"Nothing has happened yet, but this doesn't feel good." The officer listened and took notes but had no cause for follow-up. So the church leaders had taken it upon themselves to tell William to stay away. That action, which was no doubt necessary, grieved Stephanie. She felt caught between the pathos of the situation as William probably saw it and her own sense of vulnerability.

On the Sunday morning that Stephanie discovered William in the sanctuary so early, she felt rattled and frightened. She knew one thing for sure. She couldn't concentrate with him in that pew. His presence left her quivery and full of self-doubt, the words for baptism scrubbed from her memory.

Stephanie alerted the senior pastor that William was in the sanctuary, then shut herself in her study. She told herself that her colleague could handle it and that she should focus on her duties, the baptismal liturgy and sermon.

When the service was over, others told her what happened. The senior pastor had called the police, who arrived quickly. William protested, "I just want to go to church." The officers told him, "There are plenty of other churches. You're banned from this one." They used that word, *banned*. William resisted, but limply, as they led him away.

Hearing all this, Stephanie felt troubled. She was sure William's behavior was connected to the atmosphere in the soup kitchen, but she didn't know what to do about it.

WHO ARE YOU? NUMBERS

In the book of Numbers, the Israelites are wandering in the wilderness, as they have been for decades. The leaders, Moses and Aaron, are having difficulties with the people, who keep complaining. They also disobey sacred laws. They worship false gods. Jockey for power.

A rebel group led by a man named Korah had attempted to take over the leadership of the priestly clan. God put down the rebellion, but the whole business was ghastly. Hundreds of people were swallowed when the earth opened beneath them, 250 more were consumed by fire from heaven, and 14,700 people died by plague. The whole tribe would have perished had Aaron not swooped in with a censer to make atonement and soothe the Lord's wrath (see Numbers 16).

The book is called Numbers for a reason. Besides tallying the number of people who died by various calamities, the pages also record census numbers divided by clan. Reading these chapters is a reminder of the importance of lineage. As an Israelite, who you were—or could ever become—depended on your position in your family, your family's position in the clan, and your clan's position in the tribe. Your lineage established everything about you that mattered. It was your pedigree and your power.

WHO ARE YOU? THE SOUP KITCHEN

The king of the soup kitchen at Stephanie's church was Big Joe. His name fit. He wore an enormous white apron and treated everyone like family. Big Joe had volunteered since the soup kitchen's modest beginnings. As the ministry grew over the years, so had the scope of his responsibilities. Now Big Joe held the title of director even though he, like everyone else, was unpaid.

The soup kitchen had many regulars, both clients and volunteers. Girl Scout troops, confirmation classes, students who needed to earn service hours for school—at some point they all streamed into the soup kitchen to slice vegetables, assemble sandwiches, or bake sweet treats. On any given Saturday a mix of people would be at work: sixteen-year-old girls wearing lululemon leggings, a men's group sporting Chicago Bears jerseys, or senior women in seasonally decorated sweatshirts. In the controlled chaos of the kitchen, everyone had a task presided over by Big Joe.

Big Joe was affable, calling the men "Buddy" and the women "Honey," or sometimes, "Sweet Cheeks." He liked to play the radio loud and do dance moves while waving his ladle around. The clients loved Big Joe. He dished out oversized meal portions along with out-of-bounds jokes. He liked to gather the men in a group and tell a dirty joke in a stage whisper, delighting in their guffaws. With the laughter still rumbling, he'd pull in some unsuspecting female—a teenager carrying a butter tub, or a senior citizen with a spatula, or Stephanie (if she happened to be nearby)—and repeat the joke, complete with winks at the assembled men. If the woman squirmed or looked uncomfortable, Big Joe only laughed harder. The fact that the kitchen was never empty gave his crass words a safety margin. Who would misbehave in front of so many witnesses? Plus the everpresent noise made it hard to be sure that you heard correctly. The whole situation offered plausible deniability.

Once when Stephanie was passing by the broom closet, out of sight of other people, Big Joe blocked her way, grabbed her wrists, and planted his mouth on her cheek. When she pulled away, he laughed, saying she shouldn't be rattled by a friendly greeting. But it wasn't a greeting. It was a grabbing.

As Stephanie studied the news snippet about William that Monday morning—*banned*—she kept flashing back to Big Joe's actions by the broom closet. In fact, the events with

William were causing her to rethink all the soup kitchen dynamics. When she first began as associate pastor, she thought Big Joe's approach made him perfect for his job. The clients were at ease with him, and that seemed paramount. But now she saw the situation differently.

William, like many of the clients, was vulnerable. Other than his physical size, he was a person without power. Unable to fend for himself, he depended on others. Unable to communicate well, he had little voice. His behavior toward Stephanie had been frightening, but she didn't think it was malicious, at least not intentionally so. His actions needed to be curtailed, but Stephanie didn't believe William set out to hurt her. It was easy for her to regard William as a victim too—a victim of his own vulnerability.

Where had the impressionable William learned that it was acceptable to accost women and ignore their discomfort? That behavior was routinely modeled by Big Joe at the soup kitchen. William needed a helping of life skills as surely as he needed soup and a sandwich. But instead, he'd been taught to disrespect women and invade their boundaries. When he acted on that lesson, he'd been banned from the church community.

Stephanie suddenly saw the whole situation as tragic and unnecessary, the ripple effects of one man's actions. Big Joe had created an environment that served no one except himself. That he got away with this bad behavior in the name of Jesus was a further insult.

FIVE SISTERS

Numbers 27 features five sisters whose father, Zelophehad, has just died. It's unusual and noteworthy that Scripture records their names: Mahlah, Noah, Hoglah, Milcah, and Tirzah (see Numbers 27:1).

According to the ancestral laws of this patriarchal society, property passes from father to son. If there are no sons, the property passes to male relatives. Since Zelophehad had no sons, his property will revert to his brothers and their sons. His family name will come to an end.

To the five sisters, the laws don't seem fair. Their father was a righteous man. At the very least, his portion should carry on, even if his name cannot. In Numbers 27:2, the daughters feel strongly enough to approach Moses and the other leaders to make their case. They would like to inherit their (non-existent) brother's portion of their father's property. It's a pretty gutsy ask.

When I imagine the scene, I picture a couple hundred people inside a large tent. Moses and Eleazar might be on some kind of platform. The five sisters approach. If Zelophehad's widow is still alive, she would probably accompany her daughters. But what about husbands? It seems unlikely that all five sisters were unmarried since they were mature enough to execute this plan. But the text conspicuously omits that detail. And what about other family members—the uncles and male cousins who have a stake in Zelophehad's property. Did they show up in support? The sisters must have been planning this for years. Did they tell their father the plan before he died, to get his blessing? And how did they decide who would do the talking?

Maybe I'm intrigued because I'm one of four sisters myself. We have a brother, so there are five of us in all. It makes me wonder which sister acted as spokesperson. Was it the bossy eldest? The high-achieving second? The diplomatic third, the middle child? Or number four, the family mascot? Certainly not the cutesy-pie youngest. While it would make sense to assume that the oldest daughter spoke, I might put my money on number two. The Pentateuch has a tradition of second-born siblings usurping the power of the eldest.

Whoever does the talking, the sisters first establish that their father wasn't one of the trouble-makers in that Korah rebellion. Their father's name is righteous. When Zelophehad died, he wasn't dying for anyone's sin but his own. Once the sisters make that clear, they make a straightforward appeal for fair treatment: "Our father died in the wilderness; he was not among the company of those who gathered themselves together against the LORD in the company of Korah, but died for his own sin; and he had no sons. Why should the name of our father be taken away from his clan because he had no son? Give to us a possession among our father's brothers" (Numbers 27:3-4).

"Give to us," they say. These daughters are daring. They not only address Moses and Eleazar directly, they use an imperative, a command. Perhaps the strength of their number fuels them. Perhaps they know they raise a reasonable objection, even if it contradicts sacrosanct law. Perhaps they know that their relatives won't object. Whatever the reason for their daring, they state their claim without qualifiers.

Simple fairness is a persuasive argument, and Moses is persuaded. He promises to take the matter up with God. The Lord doesn't deliberate long before weighing in with a reversal of previous law: "Moses brought their case before the LORD. And the LORD spoke to Moses, saying: The daughters of Zelophehad are right in what they are saying; you shall indeed let them possess an inheritance among their father's brothers and pass the inheritance of their father on to them" (Numbers 27:5-7).

A CONFRONTATION

During the long, dark days of winter, Stephanie attended a week of continuing education with the Young Clergy Women's Project. At that event, she had time and space to tell her colleagues what happened in the soup kitchen. Their responses confirmed that Big Joe's behavior was out of line. Telling dirty jokes was not okay. Laughing at someone's discomfort was not okay. Kissing someone without consent was not okay.

Stephanie felt buttressed by the group and formulated a plan to confront Big Joe when she returned to work. But on her first day back, things had shifted. There'd been a break-in while she was away. People were in the church building when and where they shouldn't be. This was a frequent problem during the cold weather. In response, the church secretary had requested that everyone abide by the rules and use only the front door. She would buzz in employees and visitors and keep track of who was in the building.

Disregarding that request, Big Joe used his key to come in a back entrance, bringing along a number of homeless men. The secretary heard them pushing around furniture and told Stephanie. As a pastor, would Stephanie speak to Big Joe? So Stephanie reminded Big Joe of the rules and the reasons they were important, including the safety of the staff.

Before she could finish, Big Joe blew up: "I'm doing God's work!" He was red in the face. "You're getting in my way!" He threw his keys at Stephanie, and they hit her torso. He yelled, "I quit!" and walked out the door, summoning the men to follow.

Big Joe returned the next day, claiming he was "75 percent repentant." He wanted his job back. But the church leaders had already accepted his resignation. Throwing a heavy key-ring at

Stephanie could be considered assault, and the incident took place on church property, so they held their ground. Big Joe's anger escalated until law enforcement got involved. The situation ended with a police order to keep Big Joe out of the building.

Still, he had his supporters. Big Joe's friends wrote letters to the church board dissing Stephanie's ministry. Among other things, some alleged that her prayers did not reach God because she was a woman. The letters were not signed, which made them easier to ignore. Some even struck Stephanie as funny, with a childish understanding of who God is and how prayer reaches God's "ears." But underneath the absurdity of the language, Stephanie recognized that the barbs were calculated to hurt her, a female pastor, simply because of her gender and position.

SEXISM IN A SYSTEM

Gender and position are precisely what made Stephanie a target. Her status as a clergywoman challenged the unspoken rules of sexism—that men are entitled to more power, control, respect, and authority than women. The mere fact that ordained women like Stephanie *exist* challenges these assumptions. A woman with power is maddening to someone who believes that women are inferior to men.

When sexism's central belief of the superiority of men is ignored, brutality can bristle. When it's questioned, anger can spark. When it's challenged, violence can trigger. The whole progression isn't complicated.

We see the evolution in Stephanie's story. Fortunately, she avoided a more extreme assault. There were two contributing reasons for this: she spoke up when she felt vulnerable, and church leaders and law enforcement supported her.

The dynamics between Big Joe and the soup kitchen clients illustrate how sexist behaviors infiltrate and affect a system, and how outside responses can vary. The differences in how people responded to William and Big Joe show that more powerful men (Big Joe) are usually allowed to exhibit more sexist behavior than less powerful men (William). This is the problem of impunity—the more power a man has, the more leeway he has to commit infractions and go unpunished.

Because William had a lower status, his behaviors elicited prompt responses from law enforcement. His skin color was undoubtedly a factor as well. People rally quickly to protect a woman—especially a young, college-educated, white woman such as Stephanie—from a man of low status, especially a man of color. A man with high status would be given much more latitude. Would a white man in a business suit have been evicted from the sanctuary that Sunday morning?

Big Joe was not exactly high status, but he *was* protected by his position as director of the soup kitchen. Holding a position in a church, whether paid or unpaid, clergy or lay, can grant access to the church's inner workings. Churches are not quick to revoke these privileges or expose misconduct. If not for the vigilance of the secretary—which prompted Stephanie's intervention—Big Joe would not have resigned. He might still be hoisting his ladle and chortling at dirty jokes.

Church leaders often have difficulty with terminations. Resources exist to help churches address this perennial problem.[1] Terminating volunteers is especially difficult since those relationships tend to be less formal. I'll bet a few leaders were tempted to reinstate Big Joe when folks rallied to support him by writing letters. Kudos to the church leaders for standing firm. Kudos to Stephanie for seeing the letter-writing campaign for what it was—an attempt to undermine her authority. When you're the victim of a sexist attack, it can be difficult to take in the larger, systemic picture. That's one reason these attacks are so hurtful. Aiming at sex or gender—like aiming at race or ethnicity—targets something enduring, unchosen, and deeply personal. Such attacks are both cruel and effective.

ANGER AND POWER AT WORK

Big Joe would probably deny that his behavior was sexist. He might contend that he and Stephanie get along just fine. He might add a caveat with a wink, "except when she's on the rag." Or he might say he has no respect for Stephanie for darn good reasons. Either way, he would be unlikely to examine his own actions, heart, or motivation. He would take easy refuge in blaming his problems on the shortcomings of the women around him.

Let's imagine that a church leader asked Big Joe about his relationship with Stephanie. He might bring up a number of valid issues: Perhaps Stephanie *is* overly sensitive. Perhaps she *does* need to toughen up. Perhaps she doesn't understand the plight of homeless men like he does. All of this seems unlikely in reality since Stephanie has served effectively, but let's assume Big Joe is correct. What of it? Would any of these be grounds for him to purposely make her uncomfortable? To force a kiss on her? To explode at her as she performs the duties of her position? Big Joe's likely underlying assumption is an ancient one, that a woman's body is a form of property rather than a home for her sacred self. If a woman's body does not belong to her, then why not threaten her, demean her, and treat her as subservient?

The fact that Big Joe seems unaware of these dynamics makes confronting them difficult. Willful ignorance is just that: willful. Maybe Big Joe doesn't recognize his own sexism because he disguises it. Cloaking abusive attitudes toward women in jokes and joviality is common camouflage. But jokes are too thin a whitewash to cover the slashing red stain of sexism.

Men are rarely forced to question their own anger. They simply give it voice, as if men should never have to endure the maddening feeling of being powerless. But people are often powerless. This is part of our human condition, our creatureliness, our finitude. Humans are not God. Even male humans. Humans will sometimes—often—feel powerless for a whole host of reasons. Many of the world's problems stem from the inability of males to cope with feeling powerless. Men would do well to learn the lessons that women are schooled in over a lifetime: the lessons of vulnerability.

Some of the ways that women learn to survive without power are not helpful. We learn to be seen as non-threatening, to stay small and play it safe. But we also learn to be wise, tread carefully, and watch our words and tone of voice. When we finally step into power, we are ready. We can count the costs. If our tone of voice and actions are considered provocative—not sexually provocative but power provocative—we might pay a price. But we might reap tremendous benefits. This is called finding our voice.

Look at Stephanie's actions. She tolerated the discomfort caused by William's banishment and pondered her role in that action. When the church secretary requested assistance with Big Joe, Stephanie acted as befit a pastor. She used her voice. When Big Joe, enraged, threw his keys at her chest—a gesture which was oddly fitting—Stephanie had prevailed. A ring of keys may be a handy, heavy missile, but they're also a symbol of authority. Keys open doors and grant access. They symbolize ownership. Perhaps Big Joe wanted the weight of his keys to inflict a wound, but instead he returned power to its rightful owner.

THE SISTERS PREVAIL

The five daughters of Zelophehad prevail. In fact, the Lord not only rules in their favor but also permanently changes the inheritance laws of the Israelites: "You shall also say to the Israelites, 'If a man dies, and has no son, then you shall pass his inheritance on to his daughter'" (Numbers 27:8). These sisters could not have been the first all-female family in Israel, but they were the first to challenge the laws of patrilineal descent. By raising their collective voice they change a long-standing, seemingly God-ordained law. Their courageous action positively affects the female members of their tribe for centuries to come.

The five sisters demonstrate how we can negotiate a significant change, using these four steps:

\# Draw on the power of the sisterhood.

\# Present a specific, concrete request.

\# Anchor the request in a reasonable argument.

\# Appeal to a basic principle of fairness and justice.

This brief passage in Numbers suggests correlations between strength in numbers and justice. When people raise their voices together to pursue equity, that collective voice can multiply justice for countless others.

STRENGTH IN NUMBERS

Stephanie was a single individual, yet she did not seek justice alone. She drew on the help and resources of a number of people. For instance, when she realized that William was following her, she asked her senior pastor for advice. She followed that advice and reported the situation to the police. When it became apparent that William needed to be asked to leave the church premises, Stephanie worked with the church leaders to implement that plan. When William violated that agreement and showed up in the sanctuary, she again turned to her colleagues.

Reflecting on William's situation made her wonder if he learned his bad behavior at the soup kitchen. So she turned to colleagues for reinforcement and insight at the Young Clergy Women's Project. They were faithful partners to her. In turn, Stephanie was a faithful partner to the church secretary, who was concerned about the security of the church building and its people. When Big Joe threw his keys at Stephanie, she reported the situation to the church leaders so that they could take appropriate action and terminate his position.

No single action was earth-shattering, but taken cumulatively, the actions created significant change within that church system. I daresay that taking each action was uncomfortable in the moment. It's personally challenging to raise your voice when you feel vulnerable. Persons *with* power speak up, not persons *without* power. Yet that moment of vulnerability is precisely when it's important to raise your voice. Deciding *when* to speak up and *to whom* is crucial.

Stephanie's actions—like those of Zelophehad's daughters—remind us that we do not raise our voices alone or *for* ourselves alone, even when we are pursuing our own cause of justice.

Others will benefit. Imagine what a different place that soup kitchen became when someone other than Big Joe wielded the mighty ladle. Stephanie's actions likely saved women from sexual harassment, and perhaps even spared them from sexual assault.

One of the strengths of the #MeToo movement is the rise of collective action. *Time* magazine recognized this by naming "The Silence Breakers" their "Person of the Year for 2017."[2] As survivors share their stories, their experiences are validated by others who've been in similar situations. The result is cumulative. The power grows like a rolling snowball, gathering volume, mass, and staying power. For millennia, women have adapted to sexist cultures, but now we have the means and mass to resist.

Let me mention one more thing, which may seem trivial but is not. Stephanie used her voice even though she was uncomfortably aware of the privilege she enjoyed. Instead of feeling apologetic about that privilege, she exercised it. That can be a tricky dance. But unless we learn to speak up for ourselves first—using whatever means we have at hand—we are unlikely to speak up for others who have less voice. Through practice, we learn to push through the vulnerability we feel and find our voice, join the collective voice, and amplify the voices of others.

THE TEXT ASKS US

1. What does it mean that the Lord's will is not unalterable?
2. What aspect of a leader's power comes from the Lord?

MY HOPE

My hope is that the church can listen to unexpected voices like the daughters of Zelophehad and grant them what is just.

CHAPTER EIGHT

APOLOGIES AND AMENDS

*One who injures his fellow is liable concerning him
for five categories [of payment]: damages, pain,
healthcare, unemployment, and shame.*

MISHNAH BAVA KAMMA 8:1

*It would be better for you if a great millstone were fastened
around your neck and you were drowned in the depth of the sea.*

MATTHEW 18:6

THE MEETING ROOM WAS CAVERNOUS and tended to echo. Microphone stands dotted the aisles like sentinels. At each microphone, speakers brandished colored paddles to signal their purpose—green to support a motion, red to speak against, yellow to ask a question. Each speaker's face was projected on giant screens, creating a sense of intimacy among the seven hundred people attending the 2016 meeting of the General Assembly of the Presbyterian Church (USA). From a raised dais, officeholders managed the logistics. The stated clerk weighed in frequently as expert on rules and procedures.

On Wednesday evening, the agenda listed the next item of business: a policy to protect children, youth, and vulnerable adults.[1] The committee member who introduced the item spoke through tears: "I'm not the only one in tears. The place we gather is sacred. In part, because . . . [we] can hear the truth of the pain and brokenness of the human condition."[2]

A paragraph appeared on the giant screen: "We do this out of compassion for Kris Schondelmeyer and all other victims who have suffered abuse in the Presbyterian church. We further applaud Kris and his family for their courage, which has moved us to address this imperative subject." Another committee member thanked Kris for telling his story of violation, betrayal, healing, and hope: "We were broken open as a committee, and we want to share our love and gratitude with him and, on behalf of this body, say how much that meant for us." The motion to approve the policy passed unanimously.

A PUBLIC APOLOGY: KRIS'S STORY

Then the stated clerk rose and cleared his throat repeatedly. "The Reverend Kris Schondelmeyer is a minister in good standing in Maumee Valley Presbytery. In the year 2000, at seventeen years of age, he attended a national youth event where he was sexually assaulted by a chaperone sent by his own presbytery. It became a repressed memory, which is one of our body's ways of trying to heal ourselves. That memory came back with a force in the last few years, and Kris has fought an uphill battle to find justice and healing that he needs from his own church. . . . Religious institutions must acknowledge when they do harm in the world. As stated clerk of the General Assembly, I want to offer the Reverend Kris Schondelmeyer a public apology for what happened to him, a public apology for how hard it was for him to find justice, and a commitment that his child and my grandchild should be in a church that is safe."

The room erupted with applause as everyone leapt to their feet. The clapping and tears were cathartic. Who doesn't harbor some story of injustice that needs to be made right? By witnessing this moment, the whole assembly felt the thrill of justice realized. A ripple of righteousness filled the room like the purring of a cat.

A young woman came to the microphone to pray earnestly: "God, I come to you and confess that oftentimes when we bow our heads, it is not to pray but to turn our faces away from the suffering around us. So God, I ask you to remind us that in you we are much larger than we remember, and we contain the multitudes of your presence as we live in a fallen world. I thank you for the reality of who you are and that this is demonstrated to us on the cross, and that we can look at it and see a big mess that shows us that redemption is not always pretty, but is the most beautiful thing that we will find. . . . I ask you to give us courage, God, to use words like rape and sexual assault in the world and in our church buildings . . . so that we will not make light of it anymore . . . I ask you to remind us that repentance is not just words but a choice to change our minds. And I ask you to be present in our votes, as our polity will always reflect who you are if we allow it to."

Kris Schondelmeyer watched from the sidelines and let the applause and tears fill his heart. He appreciated the stated clerk's public apology, which was an unprecedented act. But that apology didn't change what was happening. At that very moment, an attorney working for the denomination was obstructing the investigation into his assault. An investigation panel, which had been formed expressly for that purpose, had failed to share any findings of fact. No amount of applause or apology could tie a bow on an incomplete package.

Even the invitation to address a General Assembly committee earlier in the week seemed less than benevolent, once Kris realized the legal reasoning. If Kris told his story, it was just that—his story. The details were not legal facts, whereas findings by the investigation panel could have relevance in a civil law proceeding. It was these findings that had been blocked. The invitation that appeared to be an act of compassion may well have been a ploy to sidestep liability.

DO NOT HINDER

One of Jesus' most beloved sayings is "Let the little children come to me, and do not stop them" (Matthew 19:14, also Mark 10:14, Luke 18:16). People bringing infants and children to the Teacher must have created logistical problems for the disciples. But Jesus was firm when adults restrained the children: "Then little children were being brought to him in order that he might lay his hands on them and pray. The disciples spoke sternly to those who brought them; but Jesus said, 'Let the little children come to me, and do not stop them; for it is to such as these that the kingdom of heaven belongs'" (Matthew 19:13-14).

Imagine Jesus hoisting a grimy child onto his lap. He seems unaware that the culture around him considers this child to be insignificant, a half-baked human not worth his time. Other people's agendas swirl around him, saying he has more important things to do than talk to children. He has powerful people to heal, eager crowds to address, a revolution to foment. Jesus counters with "for it is to such as these that the kingdom of heaven belongs."

While his followers argue over who will wear the biggest crown in the kingdom of heaven, the Teacher escapes again. He reappears at the edge of the crowd, near the parents and children. These little ones have no agenda for him. Picture a mother laying her infant in Jesus' arms while a shy toddler hides behind her knee. Or a father restraining a rambunctious five-year-old. Jesus knows what every parent seeks for their child: blessing.

Children weren't worth much in first-century Palestine. It's likely that the children Jesus blessed were not only barefoot and filthy but illiterate. They were expendable. Their parents loved them, there's no doubt, but a child didn't represent the sheer economic investment they often do today. No piano lessons at age three or Taekwondo at age four. No 529 college fund. Children at that time had very little utility, which makes it even more striking that Jesus so vigorously defends their worth.

"Do not stop them," Jesus says. Do not hinder them or hamper them. Do not impede their way. Do not curtail their progress. Do not restrict, restrain, or constrain them. Let the little children come to me.

PASTOR JACK WAYNE ROGERS

Kris shared with me the story of the assault that happened sixteen years before that General Assembly meeting. As a youth he attended a national youth conference called Connection 2000 held near Baltimore. A commissioned lay pastor, Jack Wayne Rogers, was Kris's chaperone, a role assigned to him by a denominational executive at the regional level.

Three other teens, including "Julia," one of Kris's close friends, also attended. According to Kris, Julia's mother knew some alarming facts about Jack Rogers's background. She sought out the executive to inform him. It turned out he already knew that Rogers had been convicted of receiving child pornography in 1992. Not only did the executive know, he defended his appointment of Rogers by saying that everyone deserves a second chance.

Julia's mother insisted that Rogers wasn't the appropriate person to chaperone youth. She volunteered to go in his place. She could use her vacation time.

The executive said she obviously didn't understand grace and forgiveness.

Julia's mother said she would tell others what Rogers had done.

The executive said she was welcome to leave the church.

Julia's mother claims that the executive then threatened to sue her if she didn't keep her mouth shut. As a new teacher, she feared he had the power to damage her reputation, so she said nothing. But before she let her daughter attend the conference, she put a few safeguards in place. She modified the transportation so that the youth would not spend an overnight on the road alone with Rogers. She also double-checked all the lodging arrangements.

In hindsight, those precautions weren't enough. Julia's mother blames herself for what happened to Kris, who is still a family friend. She regrets that she let herself be silenced.

THE GROOMING

For seventeen-year-old Kris, Connection 2000 began strong. Sitting shotgun as they drove to the St. Louis airport, he had Rogers's undivided attention. When they stopped to tank up, Rogers bought Kris his favorite snack foods. Occasionally the pastor reached over to rub the teen's shoulder. Rogers was four inches taller and many pounds heavier than Kris, who was a rather scrawny five foot six.

When the group arrived at the conference they browsed through a merchandise booth. Rogers bought each of the four youths a necklace, a large pewter-colored cross on a leather thong. He presented these gifts at devotions the first evening. Later he gave just Kris a special gift, a short, beaded necklace that the youth had admired.

Kris had serious concerns on his heart that summer. A few years before, at a church-related youth conference, he had felt called to ministry, an idea he wrestled against. Simply put, he didn't feel worthy. "Could God really use somebody like me?"

What most hampered Kris was his relationship with his father, who struggled with severe mental illness, paranoid schizophrenia. His parents had divorced when he was an infant, and Kris visited his father occasionally. He didn't behave like other dads. Kris had an early memory of his father screaming swear words when the two of them were alone. Little Kris somehow realized his father wasn't yelling at *him* but at someone who wasn't there. He stroked his father's back to calm him. Over the years, their roles were always reversed. Kris tried to accept his dad's limitations, but he craved a strong father figure who could show him love and make him feel valuable.

THE ASSAULT

At the conference, evening devotions were held in small groups, so the four youth were with their chaperone, Rogers. The instructions were simple: "Pray as if you're writing a letter to God." Julia began her prayer with "Dear Dad." When his good friend spoke those simple words, Kris felt pierced. His own image of

God had nothing to do with his father, who was so compromised. To pray "Dear Dad" struck him as unspeakably beautiful. Would he ever be able to address God with such tender familiarity? And if he couldn't, did he belong in ministry?

On the last evening, after devotions, Kris went to Rogers's room to ask him, How can I pray like that? They were sitting on the edge of the bed. As Kris recalls it, "When I was in that room with Jack Rogers, he started touching me. And he said, 'Sometimes God puts people in our lives to show us the love we're missing.'" With that, Rogers slipped his hand inside the waistband of Kris's gym shorts.

Kris pulled away and Rogers threw his burly body on top of him. With an effort, Kris pushed him off and ran for the door. But Rogers came after him and slammed him against the wall, slinging a powerful arm across the youth's neck, pressing against his windpipe and strangling him. Suffocating him. Even at the time, Kris recognized this as a practiced move. Rogers had done this before. As Kris gasped for air, Rogers hissed, "If you ever say anything, I'll make sure that presbytery never thinks you're good enough."

Kris told me, "I left that conference fearing Jack Rogers. But even more than that, thinking I had done something to let God down." Worried he had done something unforgivable, Kris thought about killing himself. Instead, he never spoke of the abuse, pushing it out of his mind.

INNOCENT OF SPIRIT

According to the Gospel of Matthew, we are not only to tolerate children but also to be *like* them, pure in heart and innocent of spirit. In Matthew 18, Jesus uses a child as an object lesson. The disciples are arguing about their future pecking order once Jesus comes into power. Jesus calls to a child, perhaps one from the fringes of the crowd, a child whose eyes follow him everywhere. He sets that child in the midst of the arguing men. Surprise stills their tongues.

> At that time the disciples came to Jesus and asked, "Who is the greatest in the kingdom of heaven?" He called a child, whom he put among them, and said, "Truly I tell you, unless you change and become like children, you will never enter the kingdom of heaven. Whoever becomes humble like this child is the greatest in the kingdom of heaven. Whoever welcomes one such child in my name welcomes me." (Matthew 18:1-5)

The teaching is classic Jesus. The words sound simple, but the idea they convey is enigmatic. We might think we understand, only to realize we don't, not really. What does it mean to become *like children*? We're not even sure what the kingdom of heaven *is*. But certainly we want to be with Jesus in that place.

HIS FATHER DECLINES

In 2006, when Kris was twenty-three, his father became sick with a rare cancer lodged in his abdominal wall. Kris had just been awarded a full scholarship to Louisville Seminary, but he gave it up and applied to a seminary in St. Louis, closer to where his father lived. Dad was still a three-hour drive away. For the next year and a half, Kris juggled his classwork and his father's care.

His dad's paranoia made everything more difficult. Dad kept switching doctors because he didn't trust them, complicating his continuity of care. Kris was frustrated but determined. During an especially busy few weeks, he moved his father into his one-bedroom apartment on campus and arranged for chemotherapy treatments nearby. That way he could drive Dad back and forth and still make it to class. When the chemo made Dad's favorite pudding taste different—poison, obviously—he demanded that Kris call the pudding company. Kris laughs when he tells me about the phone call, which must have been memorable on the other end. But Kris knew his father wanted to be taken seriously. It was another way for him to tell his dad, I love you.

In November of 2007, Kris had gall bladder surgery. He had staples in his stomach and wasn't supposed to drive, but when he got a call that his father was being transported to the hospital, he jumped into his car and was waiting at the emergency room when his father arrived. A doctor assessed the situation and offered to call in a chaplain.

Dad responded with a note of pride: "My son's a seminary student, I'll get my Jesus from him." He also spoke seriously to Kris: "Hey Bub, I just want you to know that I'm proud of you. You're going to be a good pastor. And I love you."

These were words he hadn't heard since he was a little boy. Stomach staples and all, they were worth the price he paid for them. Less than a week later, Dad died.

THE MEMORY RETURNS

After Kris graduated from seminary, he was called to an associate pastor position at a Presbyterian church in Toledo, Ohio. He met and fell in love with a woman named Abby, and they became engaged. The wedding was set for late December 2012.

The fifth anniversary of his father's death happened to fall a month before the wedding. On the night of that anniversary, November 16, Kris had his first violent flashback. While he slept, Jack Wayne Rogers pinned him against the wall. A powerful arm compressed Kris's windpipe, and a low voice hissed threats in his ear. Kris bolted awake gasping, unable to draw a breath. He did not sleep again that night.

When he had another flashback the next night, Kris was no longer able to fall asleep. Without sleep, his health and mood dropped precipitously. The spiral was so abrupt that the couple changed their plans. Instead of taking a honeymoon at a romantic B & B in Hocking Hills, Ohio, as they planned, they stayed home so that Kris could undergo a series of intensive EMDR (Eye Movement Desensitization and Reprocessing) treatments with a PhD trauma psychologist. His diagnosis was delayed PTSD (Post-Traumatic Stress Disorder).

At first Kris was skeptical of the "New Agey" EMDR treatment, which was a series of tapping movements, supposed to shift the location of the traumatic memory in the brain so that it could be reprocessed. But during the second session, the memory of assault came back with full force. As Kris struggled to breathe, the therapist said, "Ground yourself," and they paused. When they began again, the memory had lost some of its raw power. For the first time, Kris was able to gasp out some words about the assault. After a few more sessions, his sobbing began to diminish.

Eventually Kris went online to see what became of Rogers. What he discovered horrified him. Rogers was serving a thirty-year federal sentence for more counts of child pornography, impersonating a doctor, and performing an illegal sex change operation in a hotel room. He had sliced out someone's genitals, leaving the person nearly dead from blood loss.

That wasn't all. Rogers was also the lead suspect in the disappearance and suspected murder of a young man in 2001. That crime occurred less than a year after Rogers assaulted Kris at Connection 2000. As if a crime could be worse than murder, Rogers boasted in an online chatroom that he disposed of the young man's body in such a way that it would never be found. Later Kris read a news article citing that police had disturbing images of Rogers eating male body parts.[3]

Kris was not only sickened by these revelations but decimated by guilt. If he had come forward right away, could he have saved that young man's life? A buzzing guilt about what he failed to do became a new soundtrack for Kris, altogether different from the clamping silence he had known for a dozen years.

"IT BROKE MY HEART"

Kris resolved to press charges against Rogers. He needed to file those charges in the state where the assault took place, so in April 2013 he drove from Ohio to Maryland to make a criminal complaint. The detective assigned to the case opened an investigation. As a first step, he filed a subpoena with the PCUSA.

To Kris's shock and dismay, the attorney for the denomination refused to comply with the subpoena. Since it was issued by Maryland, it was unenforceable in Kentucky where the PCUSA is headquartered. The detective had limited options. Since Rogers was already in prison for life, the case was purely "historic." Repeated trips to Kentucky to pursue the case further would not be a good use of Maryland's resources.

"It never occurred to me that a church lawyer would refuse to cooperate with a criminal investigation into the sexual abuse of a youth at a church conference," Kris told me. "It broke my heart."

Which is how it came to be that Kris filed a civil lawsuit against the church he loves and serves.

STUMBLING BLOCKS AND MILLSTONES

When Jesus plunks a child into the middle of the squabbling disciples, he drives his point home. With the child still standing among them—an object lesson in the importance of welcome—Jesus' tone changes. He issues a stern warning:

> If any of you put a stumbling block before one of these little ones who believe in me, it would be better for you if a great millstone were fastened around your neck and you were drowned in the depth of the sea. Woe to the world because of stumbling blocks! Occasions for stumbling are bound to come, but woe to the one by whom the stumbling block comes! (Matthew 18:6-7)

Like a movie intercutting bucolic scenes with ominous images of the East River at night, we glimpse Tony Soprano's henchmen at work. They fasten a great millstone around the neck of a rival, then fling the laden body into the dark waters, which close silently over it. Jesus' message calls the Mafia to mind: "woe to the one by whom the stumbling block comes!" Churches, are you listening?

In Greek, *stumbling block* is *skandalon,* meaning a hindrance. Jesus notices how people hinder and hamper and impede the little ones. These *skandalon* are inevitable—they are *bound to come.* But that doesn't make Jesus scale back his remarks. Instead, his message intensifies:

> If your hand or your foot causes you to stumble, cut it off and throw it away; it is better for you to enter life maimed or lame than to have two hands or two feet and to be thrown into the eternal fire. And if your eye causes you to stumble, tear it out and throw it away; it is better for you to enter life with one eye than to have two eyes and to be thrown into the hell of fire. (Matthew 18:8-9)

Could Jesus speak more strongly? The stakes here are "the hell of fire."

Why is the church slow to recognize the presence and power of evil? Jesus warns that it takes extreme measures to be rid of it. Yet many Christians, unless they have personally encountered evil, are lackadaisical in their response.

CIVIL LAWSUIT 2014

Why was Pastor Jack Wayne Rogers, someone convicted for child pornography, allowed to serve as a chaperone for a national youth conference? Kris sought both answers and accountability. What he discovered astounded him.

The executive who dismissed the concerns of Julia's mother wasn't the only church leader who knew of Rogers's prior conviction. A committee of five or six persons had read a written statement Rogers submitted in 1996 "to explain his arrest, conviction, and imprisonment in 1992 for receiving child pornography." [4] That committee went on to approve Rogers's application to become a commissioned lay pastor. He was assigned to serve a small rural church with the caveat that he be under constant supervision by the pastor of his home church.

What's more, the executive and others subsequently approved for Rogers to chaperone the youth conference. Other individuals have said, on record, that they tried to warn church officials about the dangers Rogers posed, but their warnings were ignored.[5]

Perhaps because of this evidence, the national office of the PCUSA settled Kris's civil suit out of court. They awarded him three non-monetary requests and compensation of $35,000. About half of that amount went to Kris's attorney, and the rest funds his ongoing counseling expenses.

Kris didn't bring the lawsuit in order to reap a financial payout. But how an institution spends its money shows what it values. During this same time period (2014), the PCUSA spent a million dollars investigating the mishandling of a hundred thousand dollars. No malfeasance was found. The willingness to expend these funds shows the perceived importance of protecting the denomination's reputation as a fiduciary. But where does protecting the vulnerable rank in importance?

Kris is passionate about the three non-monetary awards the church agreed to implement. These were designed to create protections in the church for future children:

1. Create a document detailing the steps for reporting sexual abuse in the church.

2. Create a task force for safe and sacred space.

3. Agree to conduct an independent investigation into the Jack Rogers assault.

Because these requests were part of the court settlement, Kris assumed action would go forward on each item.

Soon after the lawsuit settled, Kris explored the idea of changing jobs. After four years of programmatic ministry in Toledo, he felt ready for a broader scope of responsibilities. A church in Wisconsin liked him and had arranged a second interview. Before that could occur, the chair of the search committee called Kris to cancel. An executive had vetoed the second interview citing "red flags." When Kris called the executive, he was told, "Look, Kris, I don't have to tell you what the red flags are, you're just not welcome to work in my presbytery."

LITTLE ONES

When Jesus protects these *little ones* so vehemently, who exactly is he protecting? "If any of you put a stumbling block before one of these *little ones* who believe in me, it would be better for you if a great millstone were fastened around your neck and you were drowned in the depth of the sea" (Matthew 18:6, emphasis added).

Little ones is usually interpreted to mean children. The phrase certainly includes them. But in the original Greek, the word *little* refers to more than size or age. *Little* means anyone of lesser status, such as persons without power or persons dependent on others. This includes any condition that creates vulnerability, whether that's a disability, an occupational level, or some kind of impairment. Vulnerable ones are *little ones*, deserving special protections.

The phrase *little ones* also occurs in Matthew 10 and makes for an interesting comparison. In Matthew 10, Jesus sends out his twelve disciples as apostles, first giving them ample instructions: "Take no gold, or silver, or copper in your belts, no bag for your journey, or two tunics, or sandals, or a staff; for laborers deserve their food" (Matthew 10:9-10). In short, the disciples shouldn't take anything that would act as a buffer to hardship. They should choose to function under a certain impairment as they do their work to "cure the sick, raise the dead, cleanse the lepers, cast out demons" (Matthew 10:8). Jesus also warns the disciples that they will face persecution but should have no fear. At the conclusion, he refers to the disciples—whom he has just sent into possible persecution without provisions—as *little ones*: "Whoever welcomes you welcomes me, and whoever welcomes me welcomes the one who sent me. . . . Whoever gives even a cup of cold water to one of these *little ones* in the name of a disciple—truly I tell you, none of these will lose their reward" (Matthew 10:40, 42, emphasis added).

To Jesus, vulnerability is sometimes a gift to be chosen. That's stunning. If *little ones*, by definition, are at the mercy of those with more power, what adult would choose to be *little*? No wonder the church is slow to apply this teaching.

What does this mean about the value and role of those who are vulnerable? They are more than valuable. They are key to the operation of the kingdom of God. Can we wrap our heads and our policies around Jesus' words? Or are we too busy protecting our power to stop and consider Jesus' outlandish warnings?

A WARNING ABOUT SHEEP

Sexual abuse, by definition, is the act of a powerful person preying on a less powerful person. A victim of sexual assault might be vulnerable for many reasons in addition to gender—younger age, lower position, inexperience, lack of weapon—which puts them into the category of *little ones*.

This lens is helpful as we return to Matthew 18. Verses 6-9 concern stumbling blocks and millstones. Verses 10-14 continue with instructions about *little ones* that weave into the Parable of the Lost Sheep:

> Take care that you do not despise one of these *little ones*; for, I tell you, in heaven their angels continually see the face of my Father in heaven. What do you think? If a shepherd has a hundred sheep, and one of them has gone astray, does he not leave the ninety-nine on the mountains and go in search of the one that went astray? And if he finds it, truly I tell you, he rejoices over it more than over the ninety-nine that never went astray. So it is not the will of your Father in heaven that one of these *little ones* should be lost. (Matthew 18:10-14, emphasis added)

The simple meaning of the text feels reassuring; there's no wonder it's applied to children. Jesus will leave behind the ninety-nine safe sheep in order to retrieve the little one in danger. It's a supremely comforting thought.

But the passage ends with another stern caution: "So it is not the will of your Father in heaven that one of these little ones should be lost" (Matthew 18:14). Like a warning, the bell is rung again. If you allow harm to happen to *little ones*, you are going against the will of your Father in heaven.

GENERAL ASSEMBLY 2016

At the General Assembly meeting in 2016, Kris realized that all three awards from his 2014 civil suit had been sidelined.

1. No polity document detailing the reporting procedures for victims of sexual abuse had been created.

2. No task force for safe and sacred space had been named.

3. An investigation panel had been formed to investigate the Jack Rogers assault but had done very little other than interview Kris.

When questioned, a denominational attorney explained that the new protection policy incorporated Kris's requests as it required stronger background checks. Kris found this inadequate; what put him at risk for clergy sexual abuse was not a lack of background checks. Church leaders knew a man's criminal background and still chose to entrust young people to his care.

Kris couldn't help but feel that current leaders were just as slippery. They had made face-saving promises without actually pursuing justice on a systemic level. In his bones, Kris knew that justice was the gateway to a pastoral response to his pain.

At the 2016 General Assembly, the stated clerk gave Kris a summary of findings. Kris later discovered that this was not an official document summarizing the work of the investigation panel but a single page created by a denominational attorney to pacify him. What's more, the summary minimized Rogers's assault by referring to it as "inappropriate touch." The document also blamed Kris for not speaking up sooner. That cut deep. Did the attorney not realize how devastating the abuse had been? Kris had turned to a pastor with his most vulnerable questions and in response was groped, strangled, and terrorized. Was the denomination really going to evade its responsibility in causing that abuse? Would they ignore the fact that Rogers was most likely a kidnapper, murderer, and worse?

To this day these questions lay across Kris's shoulders like an unwelcome yoke. Sometimes it's hard for him to pull his pulpit robe over that burden. How can he even stand in a Pres-byterian pulpit and preach the Word of God? How can he con-tinue to serve this denomination?

TELL IT TO THE CHURCH

As if Jesus anticipates that his words and warnings about *little ones* are likely to cause division, he segues into a teaching about handling church conflict.

> If another member of the church sins against you, go and *point out the fault* when the two of you are alone. If the member listens to you, you have regained that one. But if you are not listened to, *take one or two others* along with you, so that every word may be confirmed by the evidence of two or three *witnesses*. If the member refuses to listen to them, *tell it to the church*; and if the offender refuses to listen even to the church, let such a one be to you as a Gentile and a tax collector. (Matthew 18:15-17, emphasis added)

These instructions are both simple and difficult. Church members need to confront sin by naming it (*point out the fault*) and then move quickly to add appropriate witnesses (*take one or two others*). The word *witnesses* reinforces the importance of *seeing* what happened. Do not turn your head. Do not shut your eyes. Do not pretend the abuse doesn't matter.

If the offender remains unrepentant, then *tell it to the church*. In other words, tell the whole body. The body of Christ has no space—no pocket or cavity—to conceal secrets. Assault and harassment must be exposed. If the offender refuses to listen, love them but move them outside the church. Preferably, locked up.

MATTHEW 18 RECAP

Generally speaking, the people hurt by the church's falsehoods and obfuscations are not the ones in power but the vulnerable ones. Jesus repeatedly welcomed these *little ones* onto his lap. No doubt the disciples wished their boss would get on with the more important business of creating a new social order. When Kris raises his voice to call the church to a more vigorous pursuit of justice for the vulnerable, he is drawing on Jesus' teachings.

Step by step, Matthew 18 shows us how it's done:

First (verses 1-5), we must care for the vulnerable.

Second (verses 6-9), we must heed the warning about stumbling blocks that will become millstones.

Third (verses 10-14), we must be willing to extend ourselves for the safety of the vulnerable, like the Good Shepherd seeking his lost sheep.

Fourth (verses 15-17), we must follow the guidelines for confronting sin within the body of Christ.

SEXUAL ABUSE AND SPIRITUAL ABUSE

Abuse in church contexts is shockingly common. Church-related groups such as the Boy Scouts and youth groups rely on unpaid volunteers, which offers easy access to abusers. Yet abuse within a church context wounds victims especially deeply. Church buildings are called *sanctuaries*—sacred places—for a reason. What happens in a church context bears the imprimatur of the divine, whether or not the Divine had anything to do with what happened.

When someone has a position in a church, that role signifies them to be worthy of trust. If that person is an abuser, the disconnect between what *appears* to be true and what is *actually* true is so great that a victim might question reality. It's no wonder that Kris repressed the experience. He experienced terror.

Terror is different from fear. Fear passes as the danger passes, but terror changes the person long afterward. Part of this is due to neurobiology. This is why EMDR can work, and why trauma-informed care is so essential, because its tenets take seriously the neurobiology of trauma and treatment.[6] Church leaders need to become conversant with current models and best practices.

Yet the need to respond to the trauma of terror is anything but modern. Confronting evil is a human experience as old as Scripture. Why are church leaders—even those whose traditions offer concepts like original sin or total depravity—so often ill-equipped and unwilling to face the effects of evil and take a stand against it? Frankly speaking, such leaders are in the wrong business. They should consider another line of work in order to spare the *little ones* who need them to be strong and courageous and wise.

In addition, churches must recognize their pull toward institutional protectionism, which often happens for noble reasons. When an institution represents God's activity in the world, people feel moved to make sacrifices for it. Sometimes these are charitable sacrifices that enrich the givers' lives. But sometimes people sacrifice wrongly. Sometimes they sacrifice the truth.

Sexual abuse is an area where truth matters. As a youth, Kris had every reason to expect that his questions about a calling to ministry would be treated as precious. Instead, Jack Rogers seized the opportunity to violate that trust. Rogers was a lay pastor acting in a leadership capacity at a national, church-sponsored conference. The agenda of that conference was to encourage youth to draw close to God. When Kris's soul-baring led to abuse, the wound went soul deep. Sexual abuse fused with spiritual abuse is especially monstrous.

Though Kris was hurt and betrayed by the church he loves, he remains loyal to his ordination vows and continues to speak the truth in love. The question remains, will the church heed his voice or ignore it—yet again?

THE LETTER

Here's an excerpt from an open letter to the "Church That I Love" written by Kris in September 2018.

> I'm not suggesting that these PC(USA) leaders are evil. In fact, what I know to be true is that each one of them have served this denomination with truth and integrity for many years. But, even the best of leaders can be blinded by institutional protectionism at the expense of those who are most vulnerable. . . .
>
> Since finding my voice to speak about the violent sexual assault I suffered as a youth, I've been repeatedly ignored and cut off by colleagues and leaders in ministry. What they don't realize is that their silence cuts deeper than the sexual assault itself, because their silence communicates that this situation is somehow my fault. . . .
>
> It's easy to say, "Here's some money, now go away." But, I still live with the nightmares that are as real as if I'm still in that room and he's still touching me. I still have nights where I wake up unable to breathe because it feels like he's still choking me. I still have nights that I'm afraid for

my wife to touch me, nights where I just turn away and cry, hoping she doesn't see me, because I feel like I'm broken, when what I really want is to be close to her . . . but my body won't let me. I have to live with the reality that the first thought I had when taking my precious son after his birth to the church that I served, was, "What if I can't protect him here?" My goal is not to make the church look bad, or to be a thorn in the side of church leaders. I would rather stand WITH church leaders than AGAINST them, as we work TOGETHER to create safe and sacred space in this denomination that I love. . . .

I will not let go because I know that we as a denomination are better than this, we are wiser than this, we are holier than this. I truly love the PC(USA). If I didn't, I would have just walked away. Instead, I will keep holding on because I still believe that God is not done with us yet as a denomination.[7]

WHAT WILL HAPPEN NEXT?

The 2018 meeting of the General Assembly mandated another task force, this one for survivors of sexual misconduct. Among other things, that task force requires all presbyteries (regional geographic areas) to disclose the number of cases of sexual abuse within their midst.[8]

That task force, and the one for safe and sacred space, will report to the General Assembly of 2020, which is slated to meet in Baltimore. Kris likes to note that 2020 marks twenty years from the time he was assaulted at Connection 2000. The 2020 meeting will take place in the same locale as that fateful event. He is hopeful that real progress will be apparent.

THE TEXT ASKS US

1. Who are your little ones, and what attention do you give them?

2. Matthew 18:17 states, "If the member refuses to listen to them, tell it to the church; and if the offender refuses to listen even to the church, let such a one be to you as a Gentile and a tax collector." What is today's equivalent of a Gentile or tax collector? How should these persons be treated?

MY HOPE

My hope is that the church can put the needs of the *little ones* before the needs of those in power. This will be a radical shift.

CHAPTER NINE

LAMENTATION AND CLERICALISM

*My companion laid hands on a friend
and violated a covenant with me
with speech smoother than butter,
but with a heart set on war;
with words that were softer than oil,
but in fact were drawn swords.*

PSALM 55:20-21

*Clericalism, whether fostered by priests themselves or
by lay persons, leads to an excision in the ecclesial body
that supports and helps to perpetuate many of the evils
that we are condemning today. To say "no" to abuse is
to say an emphatic "no" to all forms of clericalism.*

POPE FRANCIS

WHEN STORIES OF ABUSE BRUISE our spirits, or when injustice breaks our hearts, we can come before the throne in lamentation—to shout, sob, weep, and wail. In lamentation we express not only anger, the first emotion to surface, but also the more tender feelings of sorrow, regret, fear, and helplessness. We bemoan the wrongs done to us. We regret the wrongs done *by* us. We mourn what's been lost.

The people of God lament throughout Scripture. The Israelites faced devastating situations that taught them to grieve not just as individuals but as a people. Lamentation was an appropriate response to captivity in Egypt, constant warfare in Canaan, and exile in Babylon. Consequently, the Torah, the books of history, the psalms, and the prophets are all permeated with laments lifted to the Almighty. Jesus' arrival does not change this pattern. In the Gospels, Jesus lifts a lament over Jerusalem itself (see Matthew 23:37). Many of the epistles bear the marks of life under persecution. The Revelation to John was written in exile (see Revelation 1:9).

For instruction on lamentation, we best turn to the psalms and the prophets: the psalmist supplies the words, the prophets provide the actions. The psalmist's words of lament range from private prayers of despair to communal liturgies of repentance. We can draw from this deep well of words when our own tongue runs dry. Or we can copy the prophets, who, like performance artists, lament through bold gestures: wearing sackcloth and pouring ashes over the head (Isaiah), dramatically dashing pottery (Jeremiah), brandishing a plumb line (Amos), and marching through a city declaring imminent destruction (Jonah). These actions not only express emotion but draw attention in a world preoccupied with the status quo.

LAMENTATION WITHIN THE SOCIAL ORDER

From its birth, the #MeToo movement has functioned as public lamentation. Sharing a hashtag on social media is a way to discover others of like mind or experience. The MeToo hashtag gathered voices to lament the prevalence of abuse, especially against women: *I stand with you. I add my outraged voice to yours.*

As #MeToo spread with such power and speed, an uncomfortable truth caught our culture's attention: women are abused more often than men because they are seen as *less than* men. This situation, which women face both individually and collectively, is lamentable. But expressing that lamentation—especially in public ways—is disruptive. It causes change. It seeks change! No wonder the movement evokes such powerful responses—both support and pushback.

Unfortunately, very few churches play a leadership role in #MeToo's public lamentation. Faith communities tend to follow particular political persuasions. That means their responses are shaped according to conventional politics rather than by theology and our shared texts. Because of this lens, raising a lament with and for the vulnerable strikes many as a political act that should be avoided, especially in church. But all lamentation, including that found in Scripture, does three things that are inherently part of the social order and hence political: it expresses emotion, exposes wrongdoing, and advocates for justice. These are positive and necessary acts, and there is ample scriptural precedent for engaging in them. Ignoring that, some church members in positions of privilege even denounce the voices raised in lamentation.

The same dynamics have long been true in the fight for racial justice—some churches raise a lament and seek change while others condemn the lamenters and seek to uphold the status quo. The reasons are complex but are often rooted in the fact that many churches identify with the dominant culture of this country. Historically some churches have been bastions of white privilege. These church traditions, which enjoy being power brokers have co-opted American exceptionalism and triumphalism. That experience of status and power squeezes out the felt need to lift a lament.[1]

PUBLIC AND PRIVATE LAMENTATION

Since the political divide is so—well, divisive—it's no wonder that churches often treat lamentation as a private matter. It's easier. Besides, it captures one truth. At some point everyone experiences the sorrow and grief of the human condition. As Shakespeare expressed it in Hamlet's famous soliloquy, it is fitting to bemoan "the heartache, and the thousand natural shocks / That flesh is heir to."[2] No matter how much power and privilege a person enjoys, we are mere mortals, and death is lamentable. Certainly churches, long the keepers of cemeteries, understand this. A graveyard is a lonely place.

Lament may include mourning over loss, but lament also goes far beyond private tears. Communal lament lifts up the wrongdoings that one group inflicts on another. Historically speaking, it is suppressed peoples who raise their voices against injustice while the powerful and privileged suppress those cries. The reason Scripture addresses lamentation to the Almighty may be that few others will listen.

But suppressing those cries is wrong. It is never faithful to silence the vulnerable, even unintentionally. This kind of silence is not sacred or useful. It does not honor survivors or the God who loves them.

The noise of lamentation *is* sacred and useful. It sounds a warning. It creates a clamor. This is how it does its job. How else can the people of God express painful emotion, expose wrongdoing, and advocate for justice? Noise and exposure are the very gifts our society needs to receive. By lifting a lament, the church can create space for those in pain, add biblical context to survivors' stories, and gather a chorus to support them.

This book is essentially a lament that sexual abuse is prevalent, and a call to action. I hope to inspire churches to stand passionately with survivors, pursue justice by prosecuting abusers, and make our faith communities safer and braver.

COMPLICITY THROUGH CLERICALISM

Churches not only fail to lament abuse but are often complicit with abusers. Only rarely is this intentional. More often churches aid and abet abusers through bad practices. The single largest channel for these bad practices is clericalism. When the clergy (clerics) who run churches are invested with too much power and authority, they have the means to cover mistakes and shelter secrets. Sometimes they even do these things from the best of motives. What they fail to comprehend is how their actions put vulnerable persons at risk. In the following stories, the clergy held specific understandings of the pastoral role and its burden of confidentiality, which skewed their decisions. These true stories were provided by Reverend James S. Evinger, who uses versions of them as case studies.[3]

A PAROLEE

Reverend Ashley Jones pastored a small congregation, her first. Her role as pastor was very important to her. One of the active members of her congregation, Jennifer, was married to Mike, who had just been paroled after serving time in prison for sexually abusing a child. The abuse didn't occur in the context of the church, and the victims were not connected to the church. Mike did not attend worship regularly. His only real church tie was through his wife, Jennifer, whose family were longtime members.

Mike's parole officer approached Jones and asked her to give Mike a job. The opportunity to show compassion and mercy to a former convict was appealing, and the church happened to need a janitor, so the timing was convenient. The parole officer's one condition was that the pastor would supervise Mike whenever he was in the building. Since the church didn't have a policy requiring background checks, and there wasn't a team involved in making personnel decisions, Jones agreed to the parole officer's condition and handled the hiring alone. She never told the church elders, the governing board, or any staff members about Mike's past. Policy did not require her to disclose the information, and the congregation deferred to her as pastor.

The church rented space to an outside daycare provider that had no knowledge of Mike's past or the pastor's arrangement with the parole officer. After a few months, Jones found it impossible to arrange her schedule so that she could directly supervise Mike. As a result, he often worked while the pastor was not in the building. What's more, he had keys so that he could come and go at will, which meant he had access to the building while the daycare was in operation.

Jones understood her role as pastor to mean she would honor her commitment to Mike and keep his past a secret. She never considered the risk that this arrangement—which depended entirely on her knowledge and presence—posed to minors in the daycare. She also failed to consider the risk management liability she created for the church. She never spoke with the church's insurance agent to ensure that their coverage would be in effect if a convicted abuser was allowed to work in the building unsupervised. That she failed to comply with the parole officer's terms significantly increased the risk to the children and also to the church's liability.

Eventually, Jones accepted a call to another church. This forced her to face the problem of communicating the situation, with all of its compromises, to others. She had not anticipated this circumstance. Before she left the church, Jones called the officers of her denomination, who supplied her with an expert consultant. That consultant advised her to fully inform the church's governing board before leaving. She did so. The elders on the board then had to handle a difficult situation they had no hand in creating.

The elders worried that terminating Mike's position would harm him but felt they had to do so anyway. As it turned out, Mike was able to increase his hours at another part-time job that actually paid more than the janitor position. Next, the elders wrestled with whether or not to inform the congregation about the situation. They worried that disclosure would hurt Jennifer, Mike's wife, but felt they must err on the side of transparency. They informed the congregation. It turned out that Jennifer was relieved to have the secret out in the open. Monitoring her husband's activities at the church had been a burden. Now she could have Mike attend worship services with her, secure in the knowledge that others would assist her with ensuring that people were safe.

The fact that Jones left her position worked to the church's advantage. Clericalism often grows over time, like a web. That web is constructed of power, authority, and, too often, secrets kept from lay leaders. Jones's departure shook the web, exposing secrets and redistributing power and authority to others who should rightly have it.

Since the reality of sexual abuse had entered the church's doors, the leaders had an opportunity to take next steps, beyond managing the immediate situation. But would they? Broaching difficult questions is hard work. For instance: How could the church atone for its mistakes? How might the church lift a lament for victims, both Mike's victims and others?

THREE STEPS OF LAMENTATION

Psalm 55 teaches the three steps of lamentation by illustration:

First, plead for God's attention.

Second, pour out your complaints.

Third, return to God with a statement of trust.

These three steps are simple but not easy. To travel the journey of lamentation is to return to God as a profoundly changed person.

The first two verses of Psalm 55 perform the first step—they ask God for attention.

Give ear to my prayer, O God;
　do not hide yourself from my supplication.
Attend to me, and answer me;
　I am troubled in my complaint. (Psalm 55:1-2)

The second verse segues into the complaint itself, as if troubles are bursting from the psalmist's heart.

The second step, the complaint, continues for a dozen impassioned verses.

I am distraught by the noise of the enemy,
　because of the clamor of the wicked.
For they bring trouble upon me,
　and in anger they cherish enmity against me.

My heart is in anguish within me,
    the terrors of death have fallen upon me.
Fear and trembling come upon me,
    and horror overwhelms me.
And I say, "O that I had wings like a dove!
    I would fly away and be at rest;
truly, I would flee far away;
    I would lodge in the wilderness;
I would hurry to find a shelter for myself
    from the raging wind and tempest." (Psalm 55:2-8)

Notice that the psalmist goes full throttle, voicing emotion so profound it gives way to metaphor—the desire to flee like a dove.

The complaint continues as the psalmist creatively suggests ways the Almighty could repay the evildoers. They were previously his friends and companions, the very ones he worshipped next to, making their treachery all the more searing. By verse 15, the psalmist is ready to see them die, to be buried in the grave, in Sheol.

Confuse, O Lord, confound their speech;
    for I see violence and strife in the city.
Day and night they go around it
    on its walls,
and iniquity and trouble are within it;
    ruin is in its midst;
oppression and fraud
    do not depart from its marketplace.

It is not enemies who taunt me—
    I could bear that;
it is not adversaries who deal insolently with me—

I could hide from them.
But it is you, my equal,
 my companion, my familiar friend,
with whom I kept pleasant company;
 we walked in the house of God with the throng.
Let death come upon them;
 let them go down alive to Sheol;
 for evil is in their homes and in their hearts.
  (Psalm 55:9-15)

Once the psalmist has gotten all that vitriol off his chest, the mood turns. It's as if the mention of Sheol, a scooped-out place in the earth, literally grounds the writer. Perhaps the psalmist realizes he has invoked punishment far beyond his control.

Verse 16 moves to the third step of lament: returning to the Lord with a statement of trust. The psalmist reaffirms that God is in control, that God will hear the psalmist's voice and redeem him. In verse 20, another complaint creeps in, as if the psalmist can't help but ask, Do you *realize*, Lord, what I've been through? Obviously, our laments do not have to be constructed in perfect order. We listen in while the psalmist works things out, catching himself in mid-sentence. Lamentation is a process. In verse 22, the psalmist voices a reminder, as if for his own ears: "Cast your burden on the LORD, / and he will sustain you."

But I call upon God,
 and the LORD will save me.
Evening and morning and at noon
 I utter my complaint and moan,
and he will hear my voice.

He will redeem me unharmed
   from the battle that I wage,
     for many are arrayed against me.
God, who is enthroned from of old,
   will hear, and will humble them—
because they do not change,
   and do not fear God.

My companion laid hands on a friend
   and violated a covenant with me
with speech smoother than butter,
   but with a heart set on war;
with words that were softer than oil,
   but in fact were drawn swords.

Cast your burden on the LORD,
   and he will sustain you;
he will never permit
   the righteous to be moved. (Psalm 55:16-22)

Eventually, the psalmist comes to the simplest sort of faith statement: "But I will trust in you." This statement is so barebones that it reminds me of a child gasping for mercy as an older sibling torments her with tickles and pokes. The psalmist essentially says to God, I give up. You win. Since you are God, I will submit.

But you, O God, will cast them down
   into the lowest pit;
the bloodthirsty and treacherous
   shall not live out half their days.
But I will trust in you. (Psalm 55:23)

LAMENTATION AS A PROCESS

Our troubles with lamentation begin if we neglect a step altogether or fail to complete the cycle. We might complain without first entering the divine presence. Or we might hold back our complaint, believing that God wants only our Sunday best, our shiny veneer, rather than our honest heart. Or we might raise a complaint but not long enough or loud enough, aborting the process before we catch the answering echo that God has heard our anguish.

We need to follow the psalmist's example in every step: consciously enter the Lord's presence. Hold nothing back. Use powerful language to tell the Lord what we see. Do not mince words. If friends betray us, curse them aloud! Then find the way back to the throne. Place our trust in God, not in ourselves, our own revenge, or our own storms of emotion. End our complaint with the psalmist's words to God: "But I will trust in you." If necessary, force those words through gritted teeth, Like whistling in the dark, we may hear and believe our own voice.

The process of lamentation will grow our hearts large enough to contain our sorrow and despair. The consolation of lamentation will turn our wounds into scars. The energy of lamentation will spur us to action.

A PROFESSOR EMERITUS

A couple in their late seventies, Frank and Janice, approached their pastor, Reverend Kristina LaPorte, with a request. Community Church was located in a county seat and the membership included faculty members from the local college. Janice was a deacon in the church while Frank, a professor emeritus from the college, was not officially a church member but participated actively with his wife. This was LaPorte's first position as pastor, and she had been serving the congregation for some three years.

The couple confided to LaPorte that Frank had been arrested by the state police and charged with the sexual abuse of a minor. The identified victim was not connected to the congregation, and the alleged abuse did not occur in the context of the church or its ministry. Frank vigorously denied the allegations and swore he would fight the charges. Both Frank and Janice were visibly distressed. When they requested the pastor's confidentiality, she promised it to them on the spot, without condition. LaPorte had learned in seminary that clergy confidentiality was essential to the pastoral role. She interpreted that to mean she should swear an oath of confidentiality and not violate her oath under any circumstances. In so doing, she would establish herself as trustworthy. In addition, this aligned with how she defined what it meant to be pastoral, a vague professional norm she prided herself as performing faithfully.

The couple continued to attend worship services. It did not occur to LaPorte that she might be exposing children in the congregation to an abuser or that she was creating a potential liability for the congregation as a nonprofit corporation under state law. She did not feel the need to seek consultation because she believed she was fulfilling her pastoral role. It never crossed her mind that the arrest was a matter of public record and would eventually be reported in the local weekly paper.

After the couple elicited the pastor's solemn promise of confidentiality, Janice began to tell the story of Frank's arrest to members of a club that was unaffiliated with the church. As the news spread, LaPorte realized she had placed herself in an untenable position. She sought outside advice. A mentor helped her take a fresh look at her pastoral role. This opened her eyes to the Catch-22 she had created: in honoring Frank and Janice's request as a way to preserve her trustworthiness, she had undermined that very quality—trustworthiness—among her elders and church members.

Eventually, the entire congregation discovered what had happened. At age eighty, Frank was convicted and went to prison. This congregation was given an opportunity to look evil in the face and respond as believers. Certainly, they lamented individually. Now, how could the pastor lead in communal lament to bring gifts of consolation and renewed energy for the church's ministry?

RETURNING TO GOD AFTER LAMENTATION

The third step of lamentation contains the nugget that is both difficult and powerful: after pouring out grief, sorrow, and even vindictiveness, the lamenter can return to God with a quiet confidence: "But I will trust in you" (Psalm 55:23).

Christians need not fear distortion, destruction, and death. These powers are finite. Evil and evildoers will perish while the righteous will live forever. Jesus' beautiful broken body is both the symbol and source of resurrection power. That broken body and spilled blood, bread and wine, is sustenance for the body of Christ living in a broken, bleeding world.

Of course, not everyone who looks on the cross sees the same thing. Some see only triumph and ally themselves with that power, however they perceive it, however they might obtain it. This grasping can translate into clericalism. Some see Jesus' wounds and find permission to let their wounds hobble them in fear forever. Some choose not to look on the cross at all.

We can resist the ways of triumphalism, pain, fear, and ignorance. The One we follow, Jesus, the suffering servant, was acquainted with grief and sorrow (see Isaiah 53:3). He not only allowed his *feelings* to be pierced but his very flesh. We are to live in imitation of the One who never refused to hear—and lift—a lamentation.

THE LESSON OF HISTORY

Raising a full-throated voice of lamentation is a challenge *for* the church and a challenge *to* the church. Lamentation demands that we examine our own complicities and become mindful of the lessons of history.

I live near our nation's capital and have visited the National Museum of African American History and Culture many times. Since that history is rooted in four centuries of race-based slavery, the exhibits begin deep underground in cramped, dark confines that evoke the brutal conditions of the transatlantic slave trade. Shackles and leg irons are displayed in tight spaces created from the timbers of an actual slave ship.

One excerpt from a journal records that the white captors seldom opened the ship's hatches because an overpowering stench rose from the hold, along with dirge-like moaning. The slave trader wrote, "Their singing . . . [was] always in tears, in so much that one captain . . . threatened one of the women with a flogging because the mournfulness of her song was too painful for his feelings."[4]

That's right. The ship captain could ferry human cargo across the ocean in unimaginably cruel containment. He could sell that "cargo" and spend the money he made from the flesh trade. But what the captain could *not* do was listen to an enslaved woman lament her cruel fate. He could not face the suffering his actions caused. He could not bear to glimpse the pain flowing from his complicity with evil.

I wouldn't be surprised if this unnamed ship captain were Christian. Many prominent Christians quoted Scripture to support their involvement in the African slave trade. Jefferson Davis, the president of the Confederate States of America, voiced a popular view when he said that "slavery was established by the decree of Almighty God."[5] The history of my own denomination, the Presbyterian Church (USA), is checkered by a schism over abolition. It's no wonder that Christians turned their heads, literally and metaphorically, from the sounds and smells coming from the hold of a slave ship.

As difficult as it may be to face the suffering we are complicit in causing, taking a long view is helpful. The National Museum of African American History and Culture reminds us that history will judge the actions of slaveholders more harshly than those individuals ever imagined. Some day the same may be true for those who subjugate women now. The church has the opportunity to be on the right side of history.

LESSONS TO BE LEARNED

Jones's story and LaPorte's story are examples of good intentions gone very wrong. Putting the vulnerable in harm's way simply because clergy want to see themselves as compassionate or trustworthy is inexcusable. We can lift up at least seven lessons.

Lesson one: Over-identifying with the clergy role causes trouble. When Jones did not involve the church elders in the decision to hire Mike, she deprived them of their rightful role as leaders. When she promised to oversee Mike's employment as janitor, she appropriated too much power. Actually, she assumed a God-like power. Who can be responsible for another person's actions? The elders, for their part, were accustomed to letting the pastor make decisions that exceeded the authority of that office.

In a similar way, when LaPorte failed to contact the state police as a resource, she prevented them from giving her information that would have guided her. She also did not seek counsel from the church leaders or her colleagues. She was highly invested in a certain conception of her pastoral role, which paid no mind to potentially serious and adverse outcomes for others.

Lesson two: Female pastors make mistakes too. Even though female pastors are generally more sensitive to issues surrounding sexual abuse, hiring a woman pastor is no guarantee that she will respond in the best or safest manner. All pastors need to be equipped through training in the prevention of abuse, followed by regular refresher courses. Jones let her compassion for a formerly incarcerated man trump her compassion for the vulnerable children he might imperil. LaPorte allowed herself to be complicit in Frank and Janice's desire for secrecy surrounding a serious crime. She could have exercised her agency by walking into the county clerk's office to read the arrest report for herself.

Lesson three: Acting solo is unwise. In ministry, pastors operating in the Lone Ranger mode are as common as crosses on hymnal covers. In part this is because pastors occupy a unique and often lonely position, which can create blind spots.

Information needs to spread through proper authority channels to increase safety and reduce liability.

Jones did not collaborate with the church elders before making the significant decision to hire someone convicted of child sexual abuse. She also did not seek outside advice. Jones had a severely limited analysis of the problem and did not fully consider the way her decision would affect others. This oversight created a serious and potentially costly blind spot.

In a similar way, LaPorte was aware that an accused sex abuser was worshiping in her congregation and did not inform the church leaders. Like Jones, she acted as if she could monitor another person's behavior and control outcomes.

Lesson four: Confidentiality becomes complicity. Disclosure rests on a continuum. At one end, information is freely shared, while at the other, it's held in strictest confidence. At some point along that continuum, confidentiality merges with secrecy, which can become complicity with evil.[6] Jones assumed that her clerical role mandated confidentiality above all else, which she interpreted strictly as absolute privacy. She did not weigh the best interests of vulnerable people and the well-being of the congregation overall. Out of her desire to exercise compassion and mercy, the pastor potentially became complicit in abuse. What she thought was mercy was really endangerment. Compassion for an offender should never become a rationale for lack of compassion for those at risk.

Likewise, LaPorte believed that her clerical role mandated confidentiality. But by promising the same, she was unable to meet the other duties of her role. Blinded by her need for the authority, status, and power of the clergy role, her unwitting and unwise promise endangered the welfare of others. It also put a great deal of undue stress on her as pastor.

Lesson five: Fiduciary responsibility is real. Under corporate law for nonprofit, religious congregations, both Jones and LaPorte were responsible for protecting their congregations from liability. In Jones's case, hiring a felon without disclosing it created liability. In LaPorte's case, being aware of the presence of an accused sex offender without taking protective steps created liability. By exposing children to potential harm, both pastors risked their churches' spiritual standing as safe and trustworthy. They also exposed their churches to potential lawsuits, which could destroy their financial future.

Lesson six: One-dimensional thinking is dangerous. Both pastors reacted to the situation from the perspective of being pastoral to the offender, ignoring potential victims. Jones was protective of Mike and therefore fearful and anxious about disclosing the truth of his past. After she left, the elders were also fearful and anxious but took the necessary steps, which led to a better outcome for Mike, Jennifer, and the congregation. Jones could have enacted these same steps but was frozen in one-dimensional thinking.

LaPorte acted as a pastor to Frank rather than to the congregation at large. Because Frank was fighting the charges, she immediately succumbed to the belief that he was innocent. This wishful thinking was inadequate to the seriousness of the situation.

Lesson seven: Don't neglect systems thinking. The body of Christ is a system. What happens in one part of the body affects —and can endanger—all the other parts. One part of the body cannot contain abuse without detriment to other parts. Both pastors hid facts that were vital to the well-being of their church's one body.

Clergy need to be aware of their congregation as an emotional system and the ways individuals may attempt to co-opt the pastor's position and power.[7] To use systems language, La-Porte became "triangulated" by Frank and Janice in at least three ways: into their marriage, between the couple and the congregation, and as an intermediary between the congregation and the community. Her weak position in these triangles left her holding a disproportionate share of anxiety, stress, and blame. She could have extracted herself from this situation by being more transparent with the truth and consulting with local law enforcement and church leaders.

THE CALL TO LAMENTATION

I cannot end this discussion without mentioning resistance to lamentation from those who say victims are making an undue fuss. Some politically conservative voices even say, without proof, that a significant percentage of assault accusations are *false*. While statistics on sexual assault are notoriously difficult to verify, a generally accepted figure is that between two and ten percent of reports may be *baseless*, which means *true but unsubstantiated*. That is altogether different than saying those reports are *false*, which means *an investigation factually proved the reported crime never occurred*.[8] In addition, fewer than four out of ten rapes is ever reported. Bottom line, many more assaults occur than are reported. Of those reported, very few are prosecuted, and still fewer proceed to conviction. Of course, false accusations do occur and are serious, which is why fair and transparent procedures need to be in place. The fact remains that false accusations constitute a much smaller problem than the prevalence of assault, as highlighted under the umbrella of #MeToo, which includes sexual harassment; sexual assault of women, children, and men; and even human trafficking.

Statistics do not dissuade those who want to discredit the movement. Predictably, backlash is creating a new kind of victim: powerful accused men who attempt to co-opt the vulnerability of victims in order to raise their own cries and garner sympathy.

Churches need to be discerning about the power dynamics that underlie lament. The body of Christ dares not turn away from voices raised in legitimate sorrow and anger. When a song of lamentation is not welcome in a sanctuary, the church has lost its moorings. The throne of God is exactly where lamentation belongs. Bring anger, bring sickness, bring betrayals, bring heartache—bring all of these into sacred space and pour them before a God who will hear and a community who will witness.

THE TEXT ASKS US

1. In what ways can a person come into the presence of God in order to express lament?

2. Are there any complaints that should not be voiced in God's presence?

3. What is the result of pouring out a complaint, and how can a person know that God has heard?

MY HOPE

My hope is that faith communities can harness the power of lamentation as a gift to victims and survivors, both inside and outside the church, and as a corrective to the tendency toward clericalism that is inherent in a clergy-run institution.

CHAPTER TEN

A WAY FORWARD

*Who is going to tell these little girls that what was
done to them matters? That they are seen and valued,
that they are not alone and they are not unprotected?
. . . You can communicate to all these little girls, and to
every predator . . . how much a little girl is worth.*

RACHAEL DENHOLLANDER (VICTIM/ATTORNEY WHO EXPOSED
LARRY NASSAR)

*I was a victim of sexual violence and you held my abuser
accountable. I was overcome with shame and your acceptance
healed me. I felt abandoned and you restored me to community.*

IMPROVISATION ON MATTHEW 25:35

ONE REASON I LOVE LIVING near Washington, DC, is that I
use the Dulles airport. It not only transports me to ordinary
places like Michigan but also, by way of its smooth efficiency,
into the future. Huge atriums are lined with glass blocks that
glow with light. The concourses connect by underground trains,
which are accessed by interlocking banks of escalators, all as
smooth and intricate as a zipper.

It's when you arrive at the gates that the illusion of precision
ends. Humans are everywhere. They tap on laptops or stare into

phones, tethered to charging stations. Some nurse a cup of coffee, others slowly draw chips from a snack bag. We are all measuring the minutes until boarding. Sometimes—not often—people fall asleep. We passers-by give them a wide berth.

Why? Why *don't* we disturb a sleeping traveler?

We let the stranger sleep because of an implicit covenant: *do no harm to a vulnerable person.* The rule is simple enough, but without it, society shatters. We understand this. Maybe we do no harm because we once missed a connection ourselves and have compassion for an exhausted traveler. Or maybe we do no harm because we want to avoid trouble with the law. Either way, the sleeping person is safe—in greater danger of missing a boarding call than of being molested.

THE GIFT OF VULNERABILITY

So why don't we honor this same covenant in our churches? *Do no harm to a vulnerable person.* For starters, we could make sure every child is safe. Next we could recognize that vulnerability is part of the human condition. Everyone needs safeguarding at times. We begin life as vulnerable infants, experience sickness or disability along the way, and if life is long, end our days in the frail state of old age. Our gender informs each of these experiences. We women spend great swaths of our lives in conditions softened by our own bodily needs or by tending to the bodily needs of others. Our sexuality is part of this package, a package at times marked "fragile." The greater vulnerability women experience around sexual assault is not some aberration—it's an essential piece of our human experience.

Christians so often pretend that ethics around sexual assault are vastly complicated, a morass of gender roles based in troves of Scripture and weighted down by centuries of tradition. We debate what consent entails, as if it were not a simple matter of showing other human beings respect, of being mindful of their vulnerabilities. Christians discuss whether a man and woman can safely be alone in a room, as if all men are not to be trusted, as if individuals cannot control themselves, as if the only two people who could possibly experience sexual attraction are a man and a woman, as if sexual attraction is deathly poison. So many of these assumptions are faulty. They show how uneasy church people are around sexuality in all its forms.

Maybe this is why the church treats sexual assault as "a women's issue." To Christians, sex somehow belongs to women the same way power somehow belongs to men. It's precisely this neat—and sinful—division that breeds sexual abuse.

Sexual assault is *not* "a women's issue." Sexual assault is a violation of the implicit societal covenant not to harm vulnerable persons. Every harm-er is a lawbreaker who should face legal consequences. Every harmed person should experience redress. Neither is sexual assault a private matter simply because it involves private body parts. If someone assaults a sleeping person in an airport, the arrest is not handled privately. Nor should this kind of harm.

Do no harm to a vulnerable person is another way to say "do to others as you would have them do to you" (Matthew 7:12, Luke 6:31).

JESUS' PARTING INSTRUCTIONS

Before Jesus left this planet, he gave his disciples explicit instructions. Since he was leaving time and entering eternity, the instructions were undated and have yet to expire. The instructions begin with a glimpse of the final exam, as it were, the Judgment:

> When the Son of Man comes in his glory, and all the angels with him, then he will sit on the throne of his glory. All the nations will be gathered before him, and he will separate people one from another as a shepherd separates the sheep from the goats, and he will put the sheep at his right hand and the goats at the left. (Matthew 25:31-33)

Once Jesus has everyone wondering whether they're sheep or goat, he spells out the grading rubric. It turns out that our final exam will focus on practical skills rather than theory:

> Then the king will say to those at his right hand, "Come, you that are blessed by my Father, inherit the kingdom prepared for you from the foundation of the world; for I was hungry and you gave me food, I was thirsty and you gave me something to drink, I was a stranger and you welcomed me, I was naked and you gave me clothing, I was sick and you took care of me, I was in prison and you visited me." (Matthew 25:34-39)

Any reader can see the pattern and riff on the theme. Let's improvise an addition: "I was a victim of sexual violence and you held my abuser accountable, I was overcome with shame and your acceptance healed me, I felt abandoned and you restored me to community."

Jesus' concluding words are famous for good reason: "Truly I tell you, just as you did it to one of the least of these who are members of my family, you did it to me" (Matthew 25:40).

OR, THE TANGIER MODEL

Or, we can continue business as usual. We can ignore the rising tide of awareness of sexual abuse and the resulting submersion of our churches. We can ignore our churches' disappearance from vitality within the larger culture. The *nones* (people who state their religious affiliation as *none*) have long been a growing demographic, but current abuse scandals are destroying Christian credibility. Revelations of abuse provide fodder for people to ignore and despise churches. Can we really blame anyone for being leery of a faith community?

Yet I see some churches borrowing the approach of the cantankerous fellows living on Tangier Island in Chesapeake Bay. These old codgers pretend they don't believe climate change is real, even as their island shrinks and sinks.[1] They don't seem concerned about the future. Maybe they're banking on timing —that they'll die before the island is under water. Their perspective puzzles me. Maybe they don't like their children all that much. Maybe they don't have grandchildren. For whatever reason, they choose to ignore the truth of what's happening and why.

A tide rising through our culture begs for the attention of our churches. That tide calls us to account for the ways we have mishandled God's good gifts of power and sexuality. If our churches continue to abuse these gifts, or to turn a blind eye when others do, our institutions will be under water. Our way of life will disappear.

Maybe the church as we know it would *rather* die than adapt. Maybe death is okay. We worship a God who specializes in life *after* death. That single fact puts us way ahead of the inhabitants on Tangier Island. Their island, once submerged, will not rise again from the waters of the bay. But if today's church must die, another *will* rise—because of who God is, not who we are. It's up to us to decide how to respond to the crisis we face.

CALL TO ACTION

I hope the church doesn't follow the Tangier model, not just because it ends in death but because it isn't faithful. Every generation must rise to the task set before it. Such is the meaning of discipleship. One of the challenges facing today's church is the need to respond to the ongoing revelations that women have been sexually victimized by men for far too long. Each of us has something to contribute to the #MeToo movement.

As I travel around the country speaking about sexual assault and faith, I am heartened by responses. New life is always available, if we follow Jesus. Scripture supplies the words we need to hear, and to speak. The story of Jesus healing the bleeding woman, for example, restores wholeness to survivors, to those who feel *less than*. The story of Nathan lifts up the power of prophetic pronouncement against perpetrators. Jesus' parable of the persistent widow encourages us to keep pounding on the door of justice.

I find that church leaders are eager to respond to sexual assault but wonder *how*. What resources must we harness? Our work falls into two broad camps: prevention and response. Conservative churches and progressive ones may have different viewpoints on the work. Do we need to adjust our theology or only our application? Matthew 25 speaks to this because practical skills flow from our theology. The text reminds us, first, to *do no harm*. Be honest about the ways our theology *has* done harm, even unintentionally. Do we sometimes treat girls as *less than* boys, women as *less than* men? Face that truth. Stop doing harm.

Every church must acknowledge that its seats are occupied by both victims and victimizers. It's time to rectify the power imbalances in church and society. It's time to do justice. These exposures and consequences are the reckoning in process. We must trust that when Jesus returns and the veil of time is pierced again, we will see the reckoning concluded.

WHAT DENOMINATIONS CAN DO TO LEAD THE WAY

Church bodies can't accurately assess their response to abuse until they gather statistics. Each denomination must establish procedures to report all cases of sexual misconduct and transparently make these statistics available to members and the media. This information will make it clear that now is the time to repent and confess shortcomings and sins.

Each denomination must vow to bring offenders to justice through criminal, civil, or ecclesiastical courts, and to support survivors in practical ways. Denominations must end the practice of using nondisclosure agreements in settlements for sexual abuse and harassment. They can end conflicts of interest by using separate attorneys for trying disciplinary cases and acting as fiduciaries. It may be that justice calls for costly settlements that are appropriate and not to be resisted.

Denominations that create and abide by ecclesiastical law can follow the lead of many states and end any existing statute of limitations for sexual crimes. Each denomination must reinforce reporting laws and mandate training about healthy boundaries.

Denominations can work with their seminaries to add courses that equip upcoming leaders, and retrain current leaders, in this work. Requiring certification or ongoing coursework can be an effective way to bring pastors on board.[2] Beware of dispensing this safeguarding work to Christian Education staff as a way to avoid the culture change that this deep work entails.

WHAT CONGREGATIONS CAN DO

Congregations must realize they already *have* a ministry to survivors: a ministry of absence. The truth is that when any necessary thing is withheld—be it food, water, or compassion—that powerful absence morphs into a presence of the opposite. In the case of sexual abuse, the absence of safeguards, accountability, and compassion can morph into the presence of evil.

As politicians have long repeated, the only thing necessary for the triumph of evil is that good [men] do nothing.[3] As World War II taught the world, the absence of response is not neutrality, but complicity. The same is true in responding to the evil of sexual abuse. I hope this is a disturbing realization for faith communities. Although, if congregations can grasp that the need to respond is inescapable, mustering that response may not seem as difficult.

Begin by telling your own story more honestly. Countless congregations tiptoe around past sexual misconduct and abuse. Holding these secrets creates harmful patterns that lead to further breakdown as church members avoid difficult topics, distrust each other, blame others, and allow bullies to flourish.

Watch your language. Words matter. It's easy to hide ugly realities with vague phrases like "inappropriate touch" or "crossed boundaries." Whenever possible, be more precise. The other day I heard a faith leader say that a youth pastor "had sex with" a sixteen-year-old. More correct: the perpetrator raped a sixteen-year-old.

Pluck the low-hanging fruit. Post abuse hotline numbers in the church restrooms. Display resources about abuse prominently in the church library. Use the hashtag #MeToo on your church signage and media. If you need a reason, observe April as Sexual Assault Awareness month or October as Domestic Violence Awareness month. Advertise small groups for victims and survivors, both gender-segregated groups and mixed-gender groups. They are a success if a single person shows up. They are worth doing if no one at all shows up! The message will have gone out: we can talk about this subject here. Keep at it.

Be ready to move beyond talk therapy and provide access to trauma-informed care. Become prepared for victims and survivors who might come to you for help. This means doing your own reading and finding qualified providers who take seriously the biology of trauma, especially its neurobiology.[4] Trauma-informed care also focuses on safety for victims, especially in situations of domestic abuse. Intimate partner violence is very common, well-hidden, and uniquely dangerous.

Become a braver space. Churches can, and should, make an effort to involve the whole congregation in ministry around sexual abuse. Hold open meetings to create a list of core values that will inform your church's response to abuse and serve as an anchor when allegations arise. This list might include things such as telling the truth, caring for vulnerable persons, and speaking about things that are unspeakable. Draw on the resources of your tradition, whether that's a particular historic emphasis, theological lens, or doctrinal viewpoint.

Besides the value of the finished product—the list of core values—is the value of the process of creating it. The community-wide meetings will spark important conversations, especially if they're structured to do so. To borrow a phrase from people working for racial reconciliation, these can be "courageous conversations."[5] Guidelines might include listening actively and attentively to others, assuming the best intentions of each other, speaking from our own experience, taking risks, extending grace, recognizing our own discomfort and resistance, and being willing to accept the impact of our words.

After your congregation learns how to hold brave conversations, continue by creating small groups where people can speak freely about the unexamined "gray areas" in their sexual lives. Remember that for everyone abused, there is an abuser. How many persons have a place to examine their sexual behavior through the lens of possible assault? If people look backward and realize they crossed lines in the past, create opportunities for confession and repentance, both communally and individually. Draw from your own tradition's deep well of liturgy, music, and sacrament.

Become a safer space. Many congregations have a protection policy. This needs to be revisited regularly by everyone who works with vulnerable populations. It should even be introduced to older children who work with younger children, framed as an expression of the church's love and care, which it is.

Similar training should be expanded into more in-depth healthy boundary training for all staff members and mandated on an ongoing basis. If your denomination doesn't provide this kind of training, excellent resources are available online.[6] In addition, every member of your church staff needs to understand that they are mandated reporters. If that isn't true according to the laws of your state, it is true in a moral sense. Every church leader, paid and unpaid, needs to know the exact steps they should follow if they suspect abuse. Make your commitments in writing, perhaps using this example:

> We will resist the impulse to handle abuse allegations "in house" and will report every allegation to law enforcement. We will report every allegation transparently to our church members, our denomination, and our larger community. We will budget resources for using outside experts for this difficult work. We will resist the temptation to treat sexual abuse and misconduct as personal sin that can be confessed in private.

Use your unique resources. Congregations have incredible assets that we sometimes undervalue. Two of these are Scripture and doctrine. Scripture is a powerful response to sexual abuse and can be used to lift up the healing role of justice. Preachers can commit to regularly addressing sexual abuse in sermons, and church leaders can publicly support this commitment. Let people know of this decision in advance, and revisit the topic regularly. In addition to sermons, sponsor Bible studies. The biblical pieces in this book and the discussion questions at the end of each chapter may be a starting point. These Bible study spaces can also become a place of courageous conversation.

Your particular church has a particular lens on the witness of Scripture. This is your theology. How do your beliefs and theological tenets shape your response to abuse victims and abusers? I know that my personal belief system has been reshaped by my experience as a survivor. I say this without embarrassment because Scripture reminds us that God is continually doing a new work in us (Philippians 1:6) and that we are working out our salvation with fear and trembling (Philippians 2:12). Grappling with abuse need not destroy your faith, but it can enrich and deepen it. As the angels remind us mortals, "do not fear."

THE FINAL BLESSING

Jesus' parting instructions were surprisingly specific as to how we should treat vulnerable ones. If we follow his instructions, we will end up at his right hand and be called *blessed*.

> When the Son of Man comes in his glory, and all the angels with him, then he will sit on the throne of his glory. All the nations will be gathered before him, and he will separate people one from another as a shepherd separates the sheep from the goats, and he will put the sheep at his right hand and the goats at the left. Then the king will say to those at his right hand, 'Come, you that are blessed by my Father, inherit the kingdom prepared for you from the foundation of the world; for I was hungry and you gave me food, I was thirsty and you gave me something to drink, I was a stranger and you welcomed me, I was naked and you gave me clothing, I was sick and you took care of me, I was in prison and you visited me.' (Matthew 25:31-36)

I have suggested that we expand these instructions to specifically include those harmed by sexual abuse. How will your church improvise on this theme? Our efforts will not go unrewarded. Jesus promises us a reward in glory: "And the king will answer them, 'Truly I tell you, just as you did it to one of the least of these who are members of my family, you did it to me'" (Matthew 25:40).

The fact that you have read all these pages means that your heart is compassionate toward those who have been abused. You are eager to do better. I thank God for you. May God grant you companions and bless your work.

ACKNOWLEDGMENTS

EVERYTHING I WRITE is inspired by love—for the Triune God, for the grace of Jesus, for my husband and daughters, for the church, for the truth.

I am grateful to the leaders of Hermon Presbyterian Church, who supported my writing vocation by granting me leave, and to Reverend Emily Rhodes Hunter, who skillfully ministered to the congregation during my absence.

I owe an extraordinary debt to those who shared their stories in the hope it would benefit others. Some are dear friends, and some I have yet to meet in real life.

- To Melissa Johnson, whose story sears me and whose resilience inspires me.

- To Ginni Richards, who courageously dares disclose her most painful mistakes.

- To Pete James and Sue Kenyon Hamblen, who have been in this for the long haul.

- To "Stephanie Green," who shows such insight and intentionality in ministry.

- To Kris Schondelmeyer, who calls for accountability in ways that continue to cost him.

Three people offered substantial critique of early drafts: Barbara Melosh, Susan Okula, and Deborah Oosterbaan. Many others, including Karin Meadows and Suzy Yoon, read early pages.

A heartfelt thanks to the members of my writing group: Lucy Bowerman, Susan Graceson, Martha Taylor, and Janet Bickel. A powerhouse of accountability and creativity!

Cheryl Prose created art pieces based on my memoir. Her creative companionship encourages so many survivors. You can view her work on Instagram and Facebook (MeToo Art Project).

I am especially grateful to James S. Evinger for his expertise over this past decade. His breadth of knowledge and generosity toward survivors continues to astound me.

I am grateful to my agent, Chip MacGregor, and everyone at InterVarsity Press, especially my editors, Al Hsu and Lisa Renninger, who believed in this book from the beginning.

This book would not exist without the support of my husband, Doug Everhart, who has never flagged in his belief that writing a book is worth the sacrifice of time and energy it requires. Our daughters, Hannah and Clara, are walking reminders that women matter as much as men.

My deepest gratitude is reserved for you readers. Our work lies ahead of us. Together we can help churches hold abusers accountable and become the beloved community for survivors of sexual abuse.

NOTES

INTRODUCTION

[1] I tell the complete story in my memoir: Ruth Everhart, *Ruined* (Carol Stream, IL: Tyndale House Publishers, 2016).

[2] For court case details, see Part 3, "The Courts," in Everhart, *Ruined*.

[3] "The Vast Majority of Perpetrators Will Not Go to Jail or Prison," The Criminal Justice System: Statistics, RAINN (Rape, Abuse, and Incest National Network), www.rainn.org/statistics/criminal-justice-system, accessed April 11, 2019.

[4] "About Sexual Assault," RAINN (Rape, Abuse, and Incest National Network), www.rainn.org/about-sexual-assault, accessed April 11, 2019.

[5] "Slavery Today," IJM (International Justice Mission), www.ijm.org/slavery, accessed April 11, 2019.

[6] EJI (Equal Justice Initiative), https://eji.org, accessed April 11, 2019; see also Bryan Stevenson, *Just Mercy: A Story of Justice and Redemption* (New York: Spiegel & Grau, 2014).

[7] Kate Manne, *Down Girl: The Logic of Misogyny* (New York: Oxford University Press, 2018), 20.

[8] Manne, *Down Girl*, 20.

[9] Kate Shellnutt, "Willow Creek Investigation: Allegations Against Bill Hybels Are Credible," *Christianity Today*, www.christianitytoday.com/news/2019/february/willow-creek-bill-hybels-investigation-iag-report.html, February 28, 2019; Kate Shellnutt, "#ChurchToo: Andy Savage Resigns from Megachurch over Past Abuse," *Christianity Today*, www.christianitytoday.com/news/2018/march/andy-savage-resigns-abuse-megachurch-standing-ovation.html, March 20, 2018; Kate Shellnutt, "Paige Patterson Fired by Southwestern, Stripped of Retirement Benefits," *Christianity Today*, www.christianitytoday.com/news/2018/may/paige-patterson-fired-southwestern-baptist-seminary-sbc.html, May 30, 2018; Sarah Eekhoff Zylstra, "More Women Sue Bill Gothard and IBLP, Alleging Sexual Abuse," *Christianity Today*, www.christianitytoday.com/news/2016/january/more-women-sue-bill-gothard-iblp-alleging-sexual-abuse.html, January 8, 2016.

[10]Robert Downen, Lise Olsen, and John Tedesco, "Abuse of Faith," *Houston Chronicle*, www.houstonchronicle.com/news/investigations/article/Southern -Baptist-sexual-abuse-spreads-as-leaders-13588038.php, February 10, 2019.

[11]Kate Shellnutt, "C. J. Mahaney Withdraws from T4G," *Christianity Today*, www.christianitytoday.com/news/2018/march/cj-mahaney-withdraws -t4g-conference-sgm-rachael-denhollande.html, March 7, 2019; and Naaman Zhou, "Sexual Abuse Victim Pursues Hillsong's Brian Houston over Crimes of His Father," *The Guardian*, www.theguardian.com /world/2018/nov/19/sex-abuse-victim-pursues-hillsongs-brian-houston -over-crimes-of-his-father, November 19, 2018.

[12]See Carol Howard Merritt, "How Our Theological Narratives Can Reinforce Abuse," *Christian Century*, www.christiancentury.org/blog-post/born-again -again/how-our-theological-narratives-can-reinforce-abuse, June 12, 2017; and Linda Kay Klein, *Pure: Inside the Evangelical Movement That Shamed a Generation of Young Women and How I Broke Free* (New York: Touchstone, 2018). Also see ongoing research by Steven J. Sandage, Peter J. Jankowski, Sarah A. Crabtree, and Maria L. Schweer-Collins, "Calvinism, Gender Ideology, and Relational Spirituality: An Empirical Investigation of Worldview Differences," *Journal of Psychology and Theology,* Sage Journals, Biola University, https://journals.sagepub.com/doi/abs/10.1177/0091 64711704500102, March 1, 2017.

1: POWER AND PATRIARCHY

[1]In the Christian Reformed Church, some prohibitions against the ordi-nation of women were lifted in the late 1990s, however, the prohibitions still exist in some congregations. See www.crcna.org/welcome/beliefs /position-statements/women-ecclesiastical-office.

[2]Betty Friedan, *The Feminine Mystique* (New York: W. W. Norton & Company, 1963), 63.

[3]Robin Morgan, *Sisterhood Is Powerful: An Anthology of Writings from the Women's Liberation Movement* (New York: Random House, 1970).

[4]I've previously shared this story in Ruth Everhart, "A Pastor's #MeToo Story," *The Christian Century*, December 4, 2017, www.christiancentury .org/article/first-person/pastors-metoo-story.

[5]See Julia Jacobs, "Anita Hill's Testimony and Other Key Moments From the Clarence Thomas Hearings," *New York Times*, September 20, 2018, www.nytimes.com/2018/09/20/us/politics/anita-hill-testimony-clarence -thomas.html.

2: SILENCE AND SHAME

[1]Based on my notes from a lecture by Amy-Jill Levine, "Teaching and Preaching About Jesus, Without Contempt for Judaism," at St. Mark Presbyterian Church, Rockville, MD, on October 26, 2017.

[2]Amy-Jill Levine, *The Misunderstood Jew: The Church and the Scandal of the Jewish Jesus* (New York: Harper One, 2006), 173.

[3]Jesus frequently discussed the law with the Pharisees when he was chastised for breaking the rules, as happened frequently (see Matthew 12:2, Matthew 15:2, Luke 19:7).

[4]For context, God sometimes "opened" or "closed" wombs as a sign of favor or disfavor (see Genesis 20:18, Genesis 29:31, Genesis 30:22, 1 Samuel 1:5).

[5]Newsbeat, "Aretha Franklin Bishop Sorry After 'Groping' Ariana Grande," BBC News, September 1, 2018, www.bbc.com/news/newsbeat-45381687.

[6]See Elizabeth Smart, *My Story* (New York: St. Martin's Griffin, 2013).

[7]Marie M. Fortune and James Poling, "Calling to Accountability: The Church's Response to Abusers" in *Violence Against Women and Children: A Christian Theological Sourcebook*, ed. Carol J. Adams and Marie M. Fortune (New York: The Continuum Publishing Company, 1995) 451-63.

[8]Judith Lewis Herman, *Trauma and Recovery* (New York: Basic Books, 1992), 7-8.

3: THE SYSTEM AND SECRECY

[1]This information and much that follows is drawn from James S. Evinger and Nan Postlethwait, with assistance from the Learning Task Force, *From Pain to Hope: Lessons from Penfield Presbyterian Church and Presbytery of Genesee Valley, 1997-2001, Regarding Sexual Boundary Violations of Minors*, report to the Committee on Ministry, Presbytery of Genesee Valley, 12/04/01. The document is available by request from the office of the Presbytery of Genesee Valley, https://pbygenval.org.

[2]Evinger and Postlethwait, with the Learning Task Force, *From Pain to Hope*.

[3]"Historic Principles, Conscience and Church Government," Constitution of the PCUSA, Book of Order, F-3.0103.

[4]I am indebted to Reverend James S. Evinger for the information and analysis in this chapter. Evinger also helped me file an accusation against Bolinger in ecclesiastical court. He maintains an annotated bibliography on clergy sexual abuse at FaithTrust Institute, www.faithtrustinstitute .org/resources/bibliographies/clergy-sexual-abuse.

[5]The Interfaith Sexual Trauma Institute is no longer active, but an archive is available at www.saintjohnsabbey.org/interfaith-sexual-trauma

-institute. Alban Institute is no longer in existence, but much of their work is continued by the Center for Congregations in Indianapolis, https://center forcongregations.org. FaithTrust Institute is based in Seattle, www.faith trustinstitute.org.

[6]National Center for Institutions and Alternatives, "Community Notification and Setting the Record Straight on Recidivism," November 8, 1996, www.ncianet.org/ncia/comnot.html, article no longer available.

[7]Evinger and Postlethwait, with the Learning Task Force, *From Pain to Hope.*

[8]Evinger and Postlethwait, with the Learning Task Force, *From Pain to Hope.*

[9]The word *pedophile* is used here according to its clinical definition in the *Diagnostic and Statistical Manual of Mental Disorders, Fifth Edition* (DSM-5). *Pedophilic disorder* refers to someone who shows "sexual desire for prepubescent children," meaning a child generally younger than age thirteen, and has acted on that interest.

[10]Robert Gomperts is currently listed on the New York State Sex Offender Registry, www.criminaljustice.ny.gov/SomsSUBDirectory/offenderDetails .jsp?offenderid=13026.

[11]Evinger and Postlethwait, with the Learning Task Force, *From Pain to Hope*, 2.

4: ACCOUNTABILITY AND JUSTICE

[1]Jesus withdraws to pray in Luke 6:12, Luke 9:18, Luke 9:28, passages which have no parallel in the synoptics.

[2]Reverend James S. Evinger maintains an annotated bibliography on clergy sexual abuse at FaithTrust Institute, https://faithtrustinstitute.org/resources /bibliographies/clergy-sexual-abuse.

[3]Email from Ruth Everhart to the investigating committee, October 12, 2010. Letter references are to the *Presbyterian Book of Order,* Rules of Discipline, which is available online at www.pcusa.org.

[4]From the Rules of Discipline: "The degrees of church censure are rebuke, rebuke with supervised rehabilitation, temporary exclusion from exercise of ordered ministry or membership, and removal from ordered ministry or membership." *Presbyterian Book of Order,* Rules of Discipline, D-12.0101.

[5]From the decision of the permanent judicial commission titled *Presbyterian Church (U.S.A.) by Geneva Presbytery v. Bolinger,* May 3, 2011. Document available at www.rutheverhart.com.

[6]Letter of the Session of Penfield Presbyterian Church to Reverend Ruth Everhart, dated August 22, 2011.

[7]Letter of the Session of Penfield Presbyterian Church to Reverend Ruth Everhart dated November 15, 2011.

5: PURITY CULTURE AND RAPE CULTURE

[1]Michele C. Black, Kathleen C. Basile, Matthew J. Breiding, Sharon G. Smith, Mikel L. Walters, Melissa T. Merrick, Jieru Chen, and Mark R. Stevens, *The National Intimate Partner and Sexual Violence Survey: 2010 Summary Report*, National Center for Injury Prevention and Control, Centers for Disease Control and Prevention, Atlanta, Georgia, November 2011, www.cdc.gov /ViolencePrevention/pdf/NISVS_Report2010-a.pdf.

[2]Emily Tillett, Kathryn Watson, and Grace Segers, "Christine Blasey Ford Concludes Testimony, '100 Percent' Sure Kavanaugh Assaulted Her," CBS News, September 27, 2018, www.cbsnews.com/live-news/brett-kavanaugh-hearing -confirmation-today-christine-blasey-ford-sexual-assault-allegations-live.

6: BETRAYAL AND DECEIT

[1]*Titanic*, directed by James Cameron (Hollywood, CA: Paramount Pictures, 1997).

[2]Josh White, "Vienna Presbyterian Church Seeks Forgiveness, Redemption in Wake of Abuse Scandal," *The Washington Post*, April 2, 2011, www.washington post.com/local/vienna-presbyterian-church-works-to-overcome-revelations -of-sexual-abuse/2011/03/30/AF3hNxQC_story.html?utm_term=.2e4ae0 700334.

[3]Josh White, "Vienna Presbyterian Church Forces Out Executive Director in Wake of Abuse Cases," *The Washington Post*, June 14, 2011, www.wash ingtonpost.com/local/vienna-presbyterian-church-forces-out-executive -director-in-wake-of-abuse-cases/2011/06/14/AGLAZ7UH_story.html ?noredirect=on&utm_term=.18abeb8175a1.

[4]Calvin College is the same college attended by the author, Ruth Everhart.

[5]Sue Kenyon Hamblen, personal letter to the congregation, June 2011. Used with permission.

7: VULNERABILITY AND VOICE

[1]One such source of resources is church consultant Susan Beaumont and Associates, LLC, www.susanbeaumont.com.

[2]Stephanie Zacharek, Eliana Dockterman, and Haley Sweetland Edwards, "The Silence Breakers: Time Person of the Year," *Time* magazine, accessed May 2, 2019, http://time.com/time-person-of-the-year-2017-silence-breakers.

8: APOLOGIES AND AMENDS

[1]The Office of the General Assembly Presbyterian Church (U.S.A.), "Presbyterian Church (U.S.A.) Child/Youth/Vulnerable Adult Protection Policy and Its Procedures," Approved by the 222nd General Assembly (2016), http://oga .pcusa.org/site_media/media/uploads/oga/pdf/child_protection_policy _final.pdf.

[2]Quotations taken from video of the meeting, "PCUSA Apology," Vimeo, June 26, 2016, https://vimeo.com/172318943.

[3]Associated Press, "Man Pleads Guilty in Botched-Sex-Change Case," Fox News, September 13, 2004, www.foxnews.com/story/man-pleads-guilty -in-botched-sex-change-case.

[4]Kris is unable to discover the identity of these persons as their names have been shielded.

[5]A letter of testimony was submitted as evidence in a disciplinary complaint Kris filed against the executive. That case was dismissed because of the time limitations of the PCUSA rules of discipline.

[6]A helpful resource is Christy Gunter Sim, *Survivor Care: What Religious Professionals Need to Know About Healing Trauma* (Nashville: General Board of Higher Education and Ministry, United Methodist Church, 2018).

[7]Kris Schondelmeyer, "A Letter to Church That I Love," *The Presbyterian Outlook,* Sept 14, 2018, https://pres-outlook.org/2018/09/a-letter-to -church-that-i-love.

[8]"GA223 Special Committees and Task Forces," Office of the General Assembly, PCUSA, accessed May 17, 2019, http://oga.pcusa.org/section/com mittees/committees/ga223-special-committees-and-task-forces/#Sexual _Misconduct.

9: LAMENTATION AND CLERICALISM

[1]See Soong-Chan Rah, *Prophetic Lament: A Call for Justice in Troubled Times* (Downers Grove, IL: InterVarsity Press, 2015).

[2]William Shakespeare, *Hamlet,* Act III, scene 1.

[3]Reverend James S. Evinger maintains an annotated bibliography on clergy sexual abuse at FaithTrust Institute, https://faithtrustinstitute.org/re sources/bibliographies/clergy-sexual-abuse.

[4]William Corbett (1806), on display at the Smithsonian National Museum of African American History and Culture, Washington, DC.

[5]Quoted in Mason I. Lowance Jr., ed., *A House Divided: The Antebellum Slavery Debates in America, 1776-1865* (Princeton, NJ: Princeton University Press, 2003), 60.

[6]See the excellent resource from Kibbie Simmons Ruth and Karen A. Mc-Clintock, *Healthy Disclosure: Solving Communication Quandaries in Congregations* (Herndon, VA: The Alban Institute, 2007).

[7]See Edwin H. Friedman, *Generation to Generation: Family Process in Church and Synagogue* (New York: The Guilford Press, 1985), and Peter L. Steinke, *How Your Church Family Works: Understanding Congregations as Emotional Systems* (Herndon, VA: The Alban Institute, 1993).

[8]"False Reporting: Overview," National Sexual Violence Resource Center, www.nsvrc.org/sites/default/files/Publications_NSVRC_Overview_False-Reporting.pdf.

10: A WAY FORWARD

[1]Carolyn Kormann, "Tangier, the Sinking Island in the Chesapeake," *The New Yorker*, June 8, 2018, www.newyorker.com/news/dispatch/tangier-the-sinking-island-in-the-chesapeake.

[2]One resource is the Insurance Board, a nonprofit corporation that serves churches mainly within three denominations: United Church of Christ, Christian Church (Disciples of Christ), and Presbyterian Church (USA). It offers, among other things, a self-assessment tool, an online self-administered inventory of a church's operations. A resource for certification is GRACE (Godly Response to Abuse in the Christian Environment) founded by Boz Tchividjian, www.netgrace.org.

[3]Often attributed to Edmund Burke, but the origin is actually unknown.

[4]A helpful resource is Christy Gunter Sim, *Survivor Care: What Religious Professionals Need to Know About Healing Trauma* (Nashville: General Board of Higher Education and Ministry, United Methodist Church, 2018).

[5]See Courageous Conversation from Pacific Educational Group, founded by Glenn E. Singleton in 1992 to help achieve racial equality in education, https://courageousconversation.com.

[6]See "Healthy Boundaries for Clergy, Spiritual Teachers, and Lay Leaders" at FaithTrust Institute, https://faithtrustinstitute.org/healthy-boundaries.

NAME INDEX